Breath, Boom

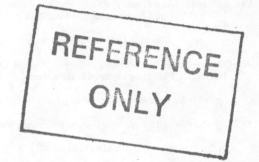

Published by Methuen 2000

1 3 5 7 9 10 8 6 4 2

First published in Great Britain in 2000 by Methuen Publishing Limited
215 Vauxhall Bridge Road, London, SW1V 1EJ

Copyright © 2000 Kia Corthron

Kia Corthron has asserted her rights under the Copyright, Designs and
Patents Act, 1988, to be identified as the author of this work

Methuen Publishing Limited Reg. No. 3543167

A CIP catalogue record for this book is available from the British Library

ISBN 0 413 75100 7

Typeset by SX Composing DTP, Rayleigh, Essex
Printed and bound in Great Britain
by Cox & Wyman Ltd, Reading, Berkshire

Caution

Breath, Boom

Kia Corthron

Methuen

ROYAL COURT

Royal Court Theatre presents

BREATH, BOOM

by **Kia Corthron**

First performed at the Royal Court Jerwood Theatre Upstairs,
Sloane Square, London on 21 February 2000

Supported by The American Friends of the Royal Court Theatre
and the Laura Pels Foundation.

BREATH, BOOM

by **Kia Corthron**

Cast in order of appearance
Prix **Diane Parish**
Angel/Correction Officer **Michele Austin**
Malika/Socks **Martina Laird**
Comet **Rakie Ayola**
Jerome **Howard Saddler**
Mother **Adjoa Andoh**
Correction Officer/Officer Dray/Fuego/Denise **Amelia Lowdell**
Correction Officer/Shondra/Pepper/Jo **Kim Oliver**
Cat/Girl/Jo's Friend **Marsha Thomason**
Jupiter **Petra Letang**

Director **Gemma Bodinetz**
Designer **Laura Hopkins**
Lighting Designer **Jenny Kagan**
Sound Designer **Paul Arditti**
Assistant Director **Dawn Walton**
Casting Director **Lisa Makin**
Production Manager **Sue Bird**
Company Stage Manager **Cath Binks**
Stage Management **Debbie Green, Julie Derevycka**
Dialect Coach **Julia Wilson-Dixon**
Fight Director **Malcolm Ranson**
Costume Supervisor **Suzanne Duffy**
Hair Styling **Joy Wallace**
Set Construction **Set-Up (Scenery) Ltd**

Royal Court Theatre wishes to thank the following for their help with this production:
Palace Theatre Watford, Devco Fireworks Ltd, Fireworks Advisor Natasha Webb, Hampstead Theatre,
Santric Ltd., Jansports (Europe) Ltd., Pepe Jeans. Wardrobe care by Persil and Comfort courtesy of Lever
Brothers Ltd. The playwright wishes to thank the New York Theatre Workshop's Dartmouth Retreat,
Audrey Skirball-Kenis and Joanne Jacobson.

JERWOOD SPACE   Subsidised rehearsal facilities provided by the Jerwood Space.

THE COMPANY

Kia Corthron (writer)
Other theatre includes: Splash Hatch on the E
Going Down (Center Stage , Yale Repertory
Theatre, New York Stage & Film, USA, Donmar
Warehouse); Digging Eleven (Hartford Stage
Company, USA); Seeking the Genesis (Goodman
Theatre, Chicago, Manhattan Theatre Club, New
York); Life by Asphyxiation (Playwrights'
Horizons, USA); Wake Up Lou Riser (Delaware
Theater Company, USA); Come Down Burning
(Long Wharf Theatre, American Place Theatre,
USA).
Radio includes: Suckling Chimera.
Awards include: National Endowment for the
Arts residency with Manhattan Theatre Club,
Kennedy Center Fund for New American Plays
for Seeking the Genesis, Young Playwrights Inc's
Joe A Callaway Playwriting Award for Come
Down Burning, Delaware Theatre Company's
First Connections Contest for Wake Up Lou
Riser, New Professional Theatre Playwriting
Award for Cage Rhythm, Van Lier Fellowship,
New Dramatists membership.

Adjoa Andoh
The Dispute (RSC / Lyric Hammersmith);
Starstruck (Tricycle); Tamburlaine, The Odyssey,
Death Catches the Hunter (Wild Iris at the
Traverse, Edinburgh); Love at a Loss (Wild Iris at
BAC); Cloud Nine (Contact); The Snow Queen
(Young Vic); Glory (Lyric/Derby Playhouse /West
Yorkshire Playhouse); Our Day Out (Birmingham
Rep); Pinchdice & Co., Lear's Daughters
(Women's Theatre Group); Getting Through
(World Tour); Twice Over (Gay Sweatshop).
Television includes: Jonathan Creek, Close
Relations, The Bill, Peak Practice, Thieftakers,
Brass Eye, Twelve Angry Men, An Independent
Man, Tomorrow People, Circle of Deceit, Health
and Efficiency, Brittas Empire, Waiting for God,
Casualty, Birthrights: West Indian Women at
War, The Missing Finger, Eastenders, I is a Long
Memoried Woman, The South Bank Show
/Glory.
Film includes: A Rather English Marriage, What
My Mother Told Me, A Prayer Before Birth, A
Short Film About Melons.

Paul Arditti (sound designer)
Paul Arditti has been designing sound for
theatre since 1983. He currently combines his
post as Head of Sound at the Royal Court
(where he has designed more than 40
productions) with regular freelance projects.
For the Royal Court: Dublin Carol, The
Kitchen, Rat in the Skull, Some Voices, Mojo,
The Lights, The Weir. The Steward of
Christendom, Shopping and Fucking, Blue Heart
(co-productions with Out of Joint). The Chairs
(co-production with Theatre de Complicite);
The Strip, Never Land, Cleansed, Via Dolorosa,
Real Classy Affair and the 1998 Young Writers'
Festival 'Choice'.
Other theatre includes: Our Lady of Sligo (RNT
with Out of Joint); Some Explicit Polaroids (Out
of Joint); Hamlet, The Tempest (RSC); Orpheus
Descending, Cyrano de Bergerac, St Joan (West
End); Marathon (Gate).
Musicals include: Doctor Dolittle, Piaf, The
Threepenny Opera.
Awards include: Drama Desk Award for
Outstanding Sound Design 1992 for Four
Baboons Adoring the Sun (Broadway).

Michele Austin
For the Royal Court: Been So Long.
Other theatre includes: 50 Revolutions (Oxford
Stage Company); Our Country's Good (Out of
Joint / Young Vic); It's a Great Big Shame
(Theatre Royal Stratford East); Fondant Fancies
and Forbidden Fruit (Old Red Lion / co-writer).
Television includes: Comedy Nation, Homie and
Away, Babes in the Wood, Skank, Kiss Me Kate,
Perfect Blue, The Bill, Frank Stubbs, Eastenders.
Film includes: Secrets and Lies, Park Stories.
Radio includes: Sweet Rugged Mystery.

Rakie Ayola
For the Royal Court: Daughters, Ashes and
Sand.
Other theatre includes: Hamlet, The Way of the
World, Macbeth, The Tempest (Birmingham
Rep); Yerma (National Theatre Studio); War
and Peace (Shared Experience / Royal National
Theatre); Each Day Dies with Sleep (Orange
Tree Theatre); Merlin, Hiawatha (Royal Lyceum,
Edinburgh); The Merchant of Venice, Mathilda,
Dracula, Up and Under, It's a Girl (Sherman
Theatre); Lord Dynamite (Welfare State); A
Midsummer Night's Dream (Moving Being).
Television includes: Voices of a Nation, Masie
Raine, Casualty, Breaking Through, Tiger Bay,
Scarlett, Soldier Soldier, A Better Life than
Mine, Night Shift.
Film includes: The Secret Laughter of Women,
Great Moments in Aviation (aka Shades of
Fear), Horse, Heart of Clay.

Gemma Bodinetz (director)
For the Royal Court: Yard Gal (co-production with Clean Break); Jack.
Other theatre includes: Hamlet (Bristol Old Vic); Death of Cool, Snake, English Journeys, Paper Husband, Chimps (Hampstead Theatre); Guiding Star (RNT/ Liverpool Everyman); Arrivderci Barnsley (Riverside Sitcom Festival); Shopping and Fucking (New York Theatre Workshop); Caravan (Bush); Dead Funny (Wolsey Theatre, Ipswich); Arcadia (tour); Dead Funny (tour); The Innocents' Crusade (Grace Theatre); Jo Jo the Melon Donkey (RNT).
Gemma Bodinetz is an associate director at Hampstead Theatre.

Laura Hopkins (designer)
For the Royal Court: Bailegangaire.
Theatre includes: Hamlet (Bristol Old Vic); Kes, Betrayal (West Yorkshire Playhouse); Ju Ju Girl (Traverse, Edinburgh Festival); Look Back in Anger, Crimes of the Heart (Royal Exchange).
Opera includes: Falstaff (Opera North); The Rake's Progress (Welsh National Opera).
With Pete Brooks: Carnivali, Plague on Both Your Houses, Clair de Luz, Blood, Peep Show.

Jenny Kagan (lighting designer)
For the Royal Court: The Madness of Esme and Shaz.
Other theatre includes: Hamlet (Bristol Old Vic); Jessye Norman 'The Sacred Ellington' (Barbican); High Life (Bush); A Small Drop of Ink (Hampstead); Things We Do For Love, An Experienced Woman Gives Advice (Royal Lyceum, Edinburgh); Starstruck, Ugly Rumours (Tricycle); Epitaph to the Whales (Gate); Measure for Measure (English Touring Theatre); Seven x 7 (West Yorkshire Playhouse); Under African Skies (Adzido Dance Company tour); Goliath (Sphinx tour); Who's Afraid of Virginia Woolf? (Almeida/Aldwych West End); Kiss the Sky (Shepherd's Bush Empire); Agamemnon's Children (Gate); Voyage in the Dark (Young Vic Studio); Moonlight Serenade (Lyric Studio); Peripheral Violence (Cockpit); Crossfire (Paines Plough).

Martina Laird
Theatre includes: Hyacinth Blue (Clean Break); The White Devil, Three Hours After Marriage, Troilus & Cressida (RSC); Venetian Heat (Finborough); Hungry Ghosts (Tabard Theatre); Vibes from Scribes (Double Edge); The Wax King (Man in the Moon); Blood Wedding (Drayton Arms); The Unlocking (Interchange Studios).
Television includes: Touch of Frost, Casualty, Always and Everyone, The Bill, Wing and a Prayer, Peak Practice, Jonathan Creek, Dangerfield, Thief Takers, The Knock, The Governor, One for the Road, Little Napoleons, Harry, West Indian Women at War, Eastenders, Epiphany.
Film includes: The Hurting.

Petra Letang
For the Royal Court: Rough Road to Survival.
Other theatre includes: The Woman Who Cooked Her Husband, Freedom is Not Free, Burglars, The Resistible Rise of Arturo Ui, Theatre in Education (Kingsway College).
Television includes: Family Affairs.

Amelia Lowdell
For the Royal Court: Yard Gal (with Clean Break), In the Family, When Brains Don't Count.
Television includes: Peak Practice, Every Woman Knows a Secret, Casualty, The Vice.
Film includes: Beginner's Luck, Essex Boys, Elephant Juice.
Radio includes: Something Blue, Not My Problem.

Kim Oliver
Theatre includes: Before the City (Vital Stages); Little Shop of Horrors (Watermill Theatre); The Children's Hour (ICA); The Bitter Tears of Petra Von Kant, Lark Rise, Measure for Measure, Love's the Best Doctor, Anna Karenina (Rose Bruford College).
Film includes: Blues is my Middle Name, Interview with the ?.
Music includes: Night Trains (European Tour); Akasha (Glastonbury Festival, St Austell Festival and Vapour '98).

Diane Parish
For the Royal Court: Sweetheart (and tour),
This is a Chair.
Other theatre includes: An Enchanted Land
(Riverside); The Birthday Party, Speed-the-Plow
(Contact, Manchester); The Tempest, Much Ado
About Nothing (Oxford Stage Company);
Hiawatha, Romeo and Juliet, Fuente Ovejuna,
Yerma, Blood Brothers (Bristol Old Vic); King
Lear (Talawa); Beautiful Thing (Duke of York's);
Generations of the Dead in the Abyss of Colney
Island Madness (Contact Theatre, Manchester).
Television includes: The Factory, The Vice 11,
Shakers, Wide Eyed and Legless, Frank Stubbs
Promotes, Complete Guide to Relationships,
Lovejoy, Holding On, Casualty, Eastenders,
Picking Up the Pieces.
Film includes: Driving Miss Crazy, Alive and
Kicking, The Final Passage.

Howard Saddler
Theatre includes: Dangerous Corner (Watford
Palace), Dead Meat (West Yorkshire Playhouse);
Our Country's Good (Young Vic / Out of Joint);
The Champion of Paribanou, Mirandolina
(Stephen Joseph Theatre); Julius Caesar (tour);
Antony & Cleopatra (Riverside Studios & tour);
She Stoops to Conquer (Bristol Old Vic); Love
at a Loss (Wild Iris tour); You Can't Take It
With You (King's Head); Titus Andronicus
(Hornsey Baths, London); Night / Silence
(Embassy Theatre Co.); Iago, Illyria (Man in the
Moon); Othello (Deconstruction Theatre); A
Man for All Seasons (The Actors Studio,
Panggung, Kuala Lumpur).
Television includes: Aquila, Meat, Grange Hill,
The Bill.
Radio includes: Love at a Loss.

Marsha Thomason
Television includes: Love in the 21st Century,
Where the Heart Is, Playing the Field, Skinny
Marink, Pie in the Sky, Prime Suspect, Brazen
Hussies.
Film includes: Priest, Safe.

Dawn Walton (assistant director)
For the Royal Court Young Writers' Programme:
Breakpoint, The Shining.
For the Royal Court as assistant director: Been
So Long.
Other theatre includes: Splinters (Talawa
Theatre Company).
As assistant director: Tamagotchi Heaven
(Edinburgh Fringe Festival '98); Hansel and Gretl
(Theatre Royal Stratford East).

THE ENGLISH STAGE COMPANY AT THE ROYAL COURT

The English Stage Company at the Royal Court opened in 1956 as a subsidised theatre producing new British plays, international plays and some classical revivals.

The first artistic director George Devine aimed to create a writers' theatre, 'a place where the dramatist is acknowledged as the fundamental creative force in the theatre and where the play is more important than the actors, the director, the designer'. The urgent need was to find a contemporary style in which the play, the acting, direction and design are all combined. He believed that 'the battle will be a long one to continue to create the right conditions for writers to work in'.

Devine aimed to discover 'hard-hitting, uncompromising writers whose plays are stimulating, provocative and exciting'. The Royal Court production of John Osborne's Look Back in Anger in May 1956 is now seen as the decisive starting point of modern British drama, and the policy created a new generation of British playwrights. The first wave included John Osborne, Arnold Wesker, John Arden, Ann Jellicoe, N F Simpson and Edward Bond. Early seasons included new international plays by Bertolt Brecht, Eugène Ionesco, Samuel Beckett, Jean-Paul Sartre and Marguerite Duras.

The theatre started with the 400-seat proscenium arch Theatre Downstairs, and then in 1969 opened a second theatre, the 60-seat studio Theatre Upstairs. Productions in the Theatre Upstairs have transferred to the West End, such as Conor McPherson's The Weir, Kevin Elyot's My Night With Reg and Ariel Dorfman's Death and the Maiden. The Royal Court also co-produces plays which have transferred to the West End or toured internationally, such as Sebastian Barry's The Steward of Christendom and Mark Ravenhill's Shopping and Fucking (with Out of Joint), Martin McDonagh's The Beauty Queen Of Leenane (with Druid Theatre Company), Ayub Khan-Din's East is East (with Tamasha Theatre Company, and now a feature film).

Since 1994 the Royal Court's artistic policy has again been vigorously directed to finding a new generation of playwrights. The writers include Joe Penhall, Rebecca Prichard, Michael Wynne, Nick Grosso, Judy Upton, Meredith Oakes, Sarah Kane, Anthony Neilson, Judith Johnson, James Stock, Jez Butterworth, Simon Block, Martin McDonagh, Mark Ravenhill, Ayub Khan-Din, Tamantha Hammerschlag, Jess Walters, Conor McPherson, Simon Stephens, Richard Bean, Roy

Williams, Gary Mitchell, Mick Mahoney, Simon Stephens, Rebecca Gilman, Christopher Shinn and Kia Corthron. This expanded programme of new plays has been made possible through the support of the Jerwood Foundation, and many in association with the Royal National Theatre Studio.

In recent years there have been record-breaking productions at the box office, with capacity houses for Jez Butterworth's Mojo, Sebastian Barry's The Steward of Christendom, Martin McDonagh's The Beauty Queen of Leenane, Ayub Khan-Din's East is East, Eugène Ionesco's The Chairs. Conor McPherson's The Weir transferred to the West End in October 1998, is now running at the Duke of York's Theatre.

The newly refurbished theatre in Sloane Square opened in February 2000, with a policy still inspired by the first artistic director George Devine. The Royal Court is an international theatre for new plays and new playwrights, and the work shapes contemporary drama in Britain and overseas.

RE-BUILDING THE ROYAL COURT

In 1995, the Royal Court was awarded a National Lottery grant through the Arts Council of England, to pay for three quarters of a £26 m project to re-build completely our 100-year old home. The rules of the award required the Royal Court to raise £7.5 m in partnership funding. The building has been completed thanks to the generous support of those listed below. We are particularly grateful for the contributions of over 5,000 audience members.

If you would like to support the ongoing work of the Royal Court please contact the Development Department on 020 7565 5000

ROYAL COURT
DEVELOPMENT BOARD
Elisabeth Murdoch (Chair)
Jonathan Cameron (Vice Chair)
Timothy Burrill
Anthony Burton
Jonathan Caplan QC
Victoria Elenowitz
Monica Gerard-Sharp
Joyce Hytner
Feona McEwan
Michael Potter
Sue Stapely
Charlotte Watcyn Lewis

PRINCIPAL DONOR
Jerwood Foundation

WRITERS CIRCLE
BSkyB Ltd
The Cadogan Estate
Carillon/Schal
News International plc
Pathé
The Eva and Hans K Rausing Trust
The Rayne Foundation
Garfield Weston Foundation

DIRECTORS CIRCLE
The Esmée Fairbairn Charitable Trust
The Granada Group plc

ACTORS CIRCLE
Ronald Cohen & Sharon Harel-Cohen
Quercus Charitable Trust
The Basil Samuel Charitable Trust
The Trusthouse Charitable Foundation
The Woodward Charitable Trust

SPECIFIC DONATIONS
The Foundation for Sport and the Arts for Stage System
John Lewis Partnership plc for Balcony
City Parochial Foundation for Infra Red Induction Loops and Toilets for Disabled Patrons
RSA Art for Architecture Award Scheme for Antoni Malinowski Wall Painting

STAGE HANDS CIRCLE
Anonymous
Miss P Abel Smith
The Arthur Andersen Foundation
Associated Newspapers Ltd
The Honorable M L Astor Charitable Trust
Rosalind Bax
Character Masonry Services Ltd
Elizabeth Corob
Toby Costin
Double O Charity
Thomas and Simone Fenton
Lindy Fletcher
Michael Frayn
Mr and Mrs Richard Hayden
Mr R Hopkins
Roger Jospe
William Keeling
Lex Service plc
Miss A Lind-Smith
The Mactaggart Third Fund
Fiona McCall
Mrs Nicola McFarlane
Mr J Mills
The Monument Trust
Jimmy Mulville and Denise O'Donoghue
David Murby
Michael Orr
William Poeton CBE and Barbara Poeton
Angela Pullen
Mr and Mrs JA Pye's Charitable Settlement
Ann Scurfield
Ricky Shuttleworth
Brian Smith
The Spotlight
Mr N Trimble
Lionel Wigram Memorial Trust
Madeline Wilks
Richard Wilson
Mrs Katherine Yates

PROGRAMME SUPPORTERS

The Royal Court (English Stage Company Ltd) receives its principal funding from the Arts Council of England. It is also supported financially by a wide range of private companies and public bodies and earns the remainder of its income from the box office and its own trading activities. The Royal Borough of Kensington & Chelsea gives an annual grant to the Royal Court Young Writers' Programme and the London Boroughs Grants Committee provides project funding for a number of play development initiatives.

Royal Court Registered Charity number 231242.

This year the Jerwood Charitable Foundation continues to support new plays by new playwrights with the fifth series of Jerwood New Playwrights. Since 1993 the A.S.K. Theater Projects of Los Angeles has funded a Playwrights' Programme at the theatre. Bloomberg Mondays, a continuation of the Royal Court's reduced price ticket scheme, is supported by Bloomberg News. This year BSkyB generously committed to a two-year sponsorship of the Royal Court Young Writers' Festival. Breath, Boom and Other People are supported by The American Friends of the Royal Court Theatre.

TRUSTS AND FOUNDATIONS
Jerwood Charitable Foundation
Laura Pels Foundation
The Peggy Ramsay Foundation
The John Lyons Charity
The Alan & Babette Sainsbury
 Charitable Fund
The John Studzinski Foundation
The Bulldog Princep Theatrical Fund
The Trusthouse Charitable Foundation

MAJOR SPONSORS
Marks and Spencer
Barclays Bank plc
Bloomberg News
BSkyB
Virgin Atlantic

BUSINESS MEMBERS
Agnès B
Cartier
Channel Four Television
Davis Polk & Wardwell
Goldman Sachs International
Laporte plc
Lazard Brothers & Co. Ltd
Lee and Pembertons
Mask
Mishcon de Reya Solicitors
Redwood Publishing plc
Simons Muirhead & Burton
Space NK
J Walter Thompson

INDIVIDUAL MEMBERS
Patrons
Advanpress
Associated Newspapers Ltd
Mrs Alan Campbell-Johnson
Gill Carrick
Citigate Dewe Rogerson Ltd
Conway van Gelder
Chris Corbin
David Day
Greg Dyke
Ralph A Fields
Mike Frain
Judy & Frank Grace
Homevale Ltd
JHJ and SF Lewis
Lex Service plc
Barbara Minto
New Penny Productions Ltd
Martin Newson
AT Poeton & Son Ltd.
Greville Poke
David Rowland
Sir George Russell
Mr & Mrs Anthony Weden
Richard Wilson
George & Moira Yip

Benefactors
Bill Andrewes
Batia Asher
Elaine Mitchell Attias
Jeremy Bond
Katie Bradford
Julian Brookstone
Yuen-Wei Chew
Carole & Neville Conrad
Coppard and Co.
Curtis Brown Ltd
Robyn Durie
Winston Fletcher
Claire & William Frankel
Nicholas A Fraser
Robert Freeman
Norman Gerard
Henny Gestetner OBE
Carolyn Goldbart
Sally Greene
Angela Heylin
Juliet Horsman
Amanda Howard Associates
ICM Ltd
Trevor Ingman
Lisa C Irwin
Peter Jones
Paul Kaju & Jane Peterson
Catherine Be Kemeny
Thomas & Nancy Kemeny
KPMG
CA Leng
Lady Lever
Colette & Peter Levy
Mae Modiano
Pat Morton
Joan Moynihan
Paul Oppenheimer
Mr & Mrs Michael Orr
Sir Eric Parker
Carol Rayman
Angharad Rees
John & Rosemarie Reynolds
John Ritchie
John Sandoe (Books) Ltd
Nicholas Selmes
David & Patricia Smalley
Max Stafford-Clark
Sue Stapely
Ann Marie Starr
Charlotte Watcyn Lewis

AMERICAN FRIENDS
Founders
Victoria & David Elenowitz
Francis Finlay
Monica Gerard-Sharp
 & Ali Wambold
Donald & Mia Martin Glickman
Carl Icahn & Gail Golden

Jeanne Hauswald
Mary Ellen Johnson & Richard Goeltz
Dany Khosrovani
Kay Koplointz
Stephen Magowan
Monica Menell-Kinberg PhD
Benjamin Rauch & Margaret Scott
Rory Riggs
Robert Rosenkranz
Gerald Schoenfeld

Patrons
Miriam Bienstock
Arthur Bellinzoni
Robert L & Janice Billingsley
Harry Brown
Catherine G Curran
Leni Darrow
Michael & Linda Donovan
April Foley
Richard and Linda Gelfond
Howard Gilman Foundation
Richard & Marcia Grand
Paul Hallingby
Herrick Theatre Foundation
Maurice & Jean R Jacobs
Sahra T Lese
Susan & Martin Lipton
Anne Locksley
William & Hilary Russell
Howard & Barbara Sloan
Margaret Jackson Smith
Mika Sterling
Arielle Tepper
The Thorne Foundation

Benefactors
Tom Armstrong
Mr & Mrs Mark Arnold
Elaine Attias
Denise & Matthew Chapman
Richard & Rosalind Edelman
Abe & Florence Elenowitz
Hiram & Barbara Gordon
Brian & Araceli Keelan
Jennifer CE Laing
Burt Lerner
Rudolph Rauch
Lawrence & Helen Remmel
Robert & Nancy Scully
Julie Talen

AWARDS FOR
THE ROYAL COURT

Ariel Dorfman's Death and the Maiden and John Guare's Six Degrees of Separation won the Olivier Award for Best Play in 1992 and 1993 respectively. Terry Johnson's Hysteria won the 1994 Olivier Award for Best Comedy, and also the Writers' Guild Award for Best West End Play. Kevin Elyot's My Night with Reg won the 1994 Writers' Guild Award for Best Fringe Play, the Evening Standard Award for Best Comedy, and the 1994 Olivier Award for Best Comedy. Joe Penhall was joint winner of the 1994 John Whiting Award for Some Voices. Sebastian Barry won the 1995 Writers' Guild Award for Best Fringe Play, the 1995 Critics' Circle Award and the 1997 Christopher Ewart-Biggs Literary Prize for The Steward of Christendom, and the 1995 Lloyds Private Banking Playwright of the Year Award. Jez Butterworth won the 1995 George Devine Award for Most Promising Playwright, the 1995 Writers' Guild New Writer of the Year Award, the Evening Standard Award for Most Promising Playwright and the 1995 Olivier Award for Best Comedy for Mojo. Phyllis Nagy won the 1995 Writers' Guild Award for Best Regional Play for Disappeared.

Michael Wynne won the 1996 Meyer-Whitworth Award for The Knocky. Martin McDonagh won the 1996 George Devine Award, the 1996 Writers' Guild Best Fringe Play Award, the 1996 Critics' Circle Award and the 1996 Evening Standard Award for Most Promising Playwright for The Beauty Queen of Leenane. Marina Carr won the 19th Susan Smith Blackburn Prize (1996/7) for Portia Coughlan. Conor McPherson won the 1997 George Devine Award, the 1997 Critics' Circle Award and the 1997 Evening Standard Award for Most Promising Playwright for The Weir. Ayub Khan-Din won the 1997 Writers' Guild Award for Best West End Play, the 1997 Writers' Guild New Writer of the Year Award and the 1996 John Whiting Award for East is East. Anthony Neilson won the 1997 Writers' Guild Award for Best Fringe Play for The Censor. The Royal Court was the overall winner of the 1995 Prudential Award for the Arts for creativity, excellence, innovation and accessibility. The Royal Court Theatre Upstairs won the 1995 Peter Brook Empty Space Award for innovation and excellence in theatre.

At the 1998 Tony Awards, Martin McDonagh's The Beauty Queen of Leenane (co-production with Druid Theatre Company) won four awards including Garry Hynes for Best Director and was nominated for a further two. Eugene Ionesco's The Chairs (co-production with Theatre de Complicite) was nominated for six Tony awards. David Hare won the 1998 Time Out Live Award

for Outstanding Achievement for Via Dolorosa. Sarah Kane won the 1998 Arts Foundation Fellowship in Playwriting. Rebecca Prichard won the 1998 Critics' Circle Award for Most Promising Playwright for Yard Gal.

Conor McPherson won the 1999 Olivier Award for Best New Play for The Weir. The Royal Court won the 1999 ITI Award for Excellence in International Theatre. Sarah Kane's Cleansed was nominated Best Foreign Language Play in 1999 by Theater Heute in Germany. Rebecca Gilman won the 1999 Evening Standard Award for Most Promising Playwright for The Glory of Living.

In 1999, the Royal Court won the European theatre prize New Theatrical Realities, presented at Taormina Arte in Sicily, for its efforts in recent years in discovering and producing the work of young British dramatists.

ROYAL COURT BOOKSHOP

The bookshop offers a wide range of playtexts, theatre books, screenplays and art-house videos with over 1,000 titles.

Located in the downstairs BAR AND FOOD area, the bookshop is open Monday to Saturday, daytimes and evenings.

Many of the Royal Court Theatre playtexts are available for just £2 including recent works by Conor McPherson, Martin Crimp, Caryl Churchill, Sarah Kane, David Mamet, Phylis Nagy and Rebecca Prichard. We offer a 10% reduction to students on a range of titles.

Further information : 020 7565 5024

FOR THE ROYAL COURT

Royal Court Theatre
Sloane Square, London, SW1W 8AS
Tel: 020 7565 5050 Fax: 020 7565 5001
info@royalcourttheatre.com
www.royalcourttheatre.com

ARTISTIC
Artistic Director **Ian Rickson**
Director **Stephen Daldry**
Assistant to the Artistic Director **Jo Luke**
Associate Directors
Dominic Cooke
Elyse Dodgson
James Macdonald *
Max Stafford-Clark *
Trainee Director **Dawn Walton****
Associate Director Casting **Lisa Makin**
Casting Assistant **Julia Horan**
Literary Manager **Graham Whybrow**
Literary Assistant **Daisy Heath**
Literary Associate **Stephen Jeffreys** *
Resident Dramatist **Simon Stephens** +
Voice Associate **Patsy Rodenburg**
International Administrator **Natalie Highwood**

YOUNG WRITERS' PROGRAMME
Associate Director **Ola Animashawun**
General Manager **Aoife Mannix**
Writers' Tutor **Nicola Baldwin**

PRODUCTION
Production Manager **Paul Handley**
Assistant Production Manager **Sue Bird**
Production Assistant **Rebecca Fifield**
Company Stage Manager **Cath Binks**
Head of Lighting **Johanna Town**
Senior Electrician **Marion Mahon**
Assistant Electrician **Simon Lally**
Lighting Board Operator TD **Andrew Taylor**
Head of Stage **Martin Riley**
Deputy Head of Stage **David Skelly**
Stage Chargehand **Eddie King**
Head of Sound **Paul Arditti**
Sound Deputy **Rich Walsh**
Head of Wardrobe **Iona Kenrick**
Wardrobe Deputy **Suzanne Duffy**
Maintenance Manager **Fran Mcelroy**

ENGLISH STAGE COMPANY
President **Greville Poke**
Vice Presidents **Jocelyn Herbert**
Joan Plowright CBE
Council
Chairman **Sir John Mortimer QC, CBE**
Vice-Chairman **Anthony Burton**
Members
Stuart Burge CBE
Martin Crimp
Judy Daish
Stephen Evans
Phyllida Lloyd
Baroness McIntosh
Sonia Melchett
James Midgley
Richard Pulford
Hugh Quarshie
Nicholas Wright
Alan Yentob

MANAGEMENT
Executive Director **Vikki Heywood**
Assistant to the Executive Director **Karen Curtis**
General Manager **Diane Borger**
Finance Director **Donna Munday**
Finance Officer **Rachel Harrison**
Re-development Finance Officer **Neville Ayres**

MARKETING
Head of Marketing **Stuart Buchanan**
Press Officer **Giselle Glasman**
Marketing Officer **Emily Smith**
Press Assistant **Claire Christou**
Box Office Manager **Neil Grutchfield**
Deputy Box Office Manager **Valli Dakshinamurthi**
Duty Box Office Manager **Glen Bowman**
Box Office Sales Operator **Gregory Woodward**

DEVELOPMENT
Head of Development **Helen Salmon**
Development Associate **Susan Davenport** *
Appeals Officer **Sophie Hussey**
Administrative & Research Assistant **Olivia Hill**

RE-DEVELOPMENT
Project Manager **Tony Hudson**
Technical Director **Simon Harper**
Assistant to Project Manager **Monica McCormack**

FRONT OF HOUSE
Theatre Manager **Lucy Dusgate**
Deputy Theatre Manager **Jemma Davies**
Relief Duty House Managers
Gregory Woodward *
Bookshop Manager **Del Campbell**
Bookshop Assistant **Sarah Mclaren** *
Stage Door/Reception **Tom Lown*, Tyrone Lucas** *,
Sophie Fox*, Alexia Smith
Thanks to all of our ushers

* part-time
+ Arts Council Resident Dramatist
** recipient of a bursary from the Arts Council of England

Advisory Council
Diana Bliss
Tina Brown
Allan Davis
Elyse Dodgson
Robert Fox
Jocelyn Herbert
Michael Hoffman
Hanif Kureishi
Jane Rayne
Ruth Rogers
James L. Tanner

Act One

Scene One

Street corner.

Prix, **Angel** *and* **Malika** *wait.* **Comet** *enters, angry. She stares at them, particularly at* **Prix**. *They stare at her.*

Comet   *What?*

She waits for them to answer. They don't.

Comet   Attitude? Don't even gimme that shit I *told*ju this is my birthday I'd appreciate the night off *please*, Toldju tonight my eighteenth big party *Ring!* shit! Get the phone. I gotta leave my guests 'Where ya goin'?' she says. 'Stuff I gotta do' and you *know* she throwin' a fit, money she put out for that damn party '*I* know where you goin'! *I* know where you goin'! Huzzy!' Ain't that a sweet way talk to your daughter only daughter her eighteenth I think but say nothin', no time to bitch with her cuz I got the damn call, know my duty I come on down here and now yaw got nothin' to say? Hop my ass down to work cuz I'm called *my* birthday, *my* eighteenth birthday, leave my friends cuz *I* got a few, desert my *friends* to meet my *sisters* and now my sisters givin' me a look like I got attitude.

She waits for them to answer. They don't.

Comet   *What?*

Prix *gives* **Angel** *and* **Malika** *a look.* **Comet** *is suddenly terrified but before she can get away* **Angel** *and* **Malika** *pounce, beating the crap out of* **Comet**: *no mercy.* **Comet** *screaming. Eventually* **Prix** *herself throws in a few kicks or punches. Boom:* **Prix** *looks up. Colored fireworks lights are reflected upon the girls.* **Prix** *stands, walks downstage, mesmerized by the lights. She says something, not loud enough to be heard over the pummeling and the fireworks. When, a few moments later,* **Malika** *realizes* **Prix** *had spoken, she pauses in her violence and indicates for* **Angel** *also to halt.*

Malika   Whadju say?

Prix (*focused on the fireworks, absently repeats*)   Don't kill her.

Having stopped the fight, **Malika** *and* **Angel** *are now aware of the fireworks. Stand, also captivated. Drawn toward* **Prix***'s area.*

Prix   What day's today?

Angel   I dunno. Memorial Day?

Prix, **Angel** *and* **Malika** *continue gazing. On the ground behind, a bleeding, near unconscious* **Comet***.*

Scene Two

Prix*'s bedroom.*

On the wall are several colored-pencil drawings of fireworks. Before the phone finishes the first ring, **Prix** *snatches the receiver.*

Prix   Yeah?

Prix *has a pencil and pad and takes notes on the conversation.* **Angel** *and* **Malika** *on the bed,* **Angel** *weaving long braids into* **Malika***'s hair.*

Malika   I don't know why Prix don't get a cell, always gotta make sure she be by her phone the right time, or by the pay phone right time. She have a cell phone she take her business with her, convenient.

Angel   She got a beeper.

Malika   *So?* People prefer a cell phone, beeper – you got the delayed action, gotta call 'em, push your number in, then wait 'til *they* find a quarter, they find a pay phone, then probably they gotta stand in line for the pay phone you know what kinda time gap that makes? Beeper, 'less it life-and-death vital, people say forget it.

Angel   Just why she say she got a beeper, she say beeper encourage 'em thus: ''less it life-and-death vital, don't bother me' Girl! I hope you know these hairs is three shades lighter 'n your natural color.

Malika   They's highlights, J.W. likes it Ow!

Angel   J.W., J.W., you know how to have a conversation without havin' to plug your damn boyfriend's name every two seconds?

Malika   Last night he bought me roses off the street and stuck one in my hair. It was real sweet 'til that thorn stabbed my scalp. Ow! I punched him and he punched me, then he goes ain't you just like Jesus, crown a thorns and we laughed and had sex and cookie dough ice cream OW!

Angel   Toldju I do it professional, professional hurts.

Malika   Wow. (*Looking around.*) Somehow I imagined Prix's room be all black, no windows. You ever been here before?

Angel   She's my cousin.

Malika   You ever been here before?

Angel   Yeah I been here before. Too many times, one buildin' away, too far for my mother get off her butt and walk but close enough she send me errand-runnin' every five minutes, 'Aunt Kerstine, Mom's done with this week's *Jet*, said you wanna read it.' 'Aunt Kerstine, my mother like to buy couple food stamps, you got some extra?'

Malika   Your mom's nice. Soft. Not hollerin' all the time I bet she never even whipped yaw.

Angel   Kiddin'? One time Darryl and me ate the cream out the Oreos, hid the hard dark part in the couch –

Prix   Okay. (*Hangs up.*) Meet at McDonald's 10:35. Car'll come by 10:45, their party's a hundred forty-first, they established a dumb routine habit a saunterin' in between 11:30 and midnight. Cruise St. Ann's, round the block. First sight a their car, hit and get out.

Malika   A'ight. Ow!

Angel   You got dandruff like nobody's business, what kinda shampoo you use?

Malika (*looking at wall drawings*) I like your fireworks, Prix.

Prix   Thanks.

Malika   My cousin rides planes sometimes. She does . . . I dunno, secretary, somethin', she wears a suit, she has business other cities, gotta take planes. She says they bring food to ya. Snack and a meal. She says them stewardesses get free flights, Spain. Africa. That's gonna be me, stewardess. High, high, winkin' down atcha from 37,000.

Phone rings. **Prix** *snatches it.*

Prix   Yeah?

Realizing who it is, **Prix** *looks at* **Angel** *and* **Malika**, *irritated. They are puzzled.*

Prix   Yeah. (*Hangs up.*) Someone buzz her in. (*Goes to her desk.*)

Malika   Who is it?

Prix *doesn't answer. Pulls from her desk various multicolored pipe-cleaner figures shaped like fireworks. After a moment,* **Angel** *interprets the silence.*

Angel   Comet.

Malika   *Comet?* I thought she was still in the hospital.

Angel (*shrugs*)   Who else made her mad lately? (*'Her' meaning* **Prix**.)

Malika   Who's mad at the people we're s'posed to hit tonight?

Angel   Not her she just followin' instructions. Nothin' personal anyway, just a drive-by, not like we shootin' anybody face-to-face. Get it.

Malika *gets up but, before she gets to the buzzer (in the hallway outside* **Prix***'s room), a knock is heard on* **Prix***'s door.*

Malika How she get in the buildin' without buzzin'?

Comet *opens the door, stands in the doorway. From the hallway: the sound of laughter, a man and a woman.* **Prix***, molding pipe cleaners into fireworks, looks up toward the door.*

Malika How you get in the buildin' without buzzin'?

Comet Prix's moms and Jerome let me in.

Prix (*turning back to her project, to herself*) Fuck.

Malika (*vague smirk*) I thought you were still in the hospital, Comet.

Comet (*entering, nervous*) Got out. Coupla days. Hi, Prix.

Angel How's Jupiter?

Comet Good! Missed me. Only two but she got a vocabulary, my mother say 'Every day that brat cryin' "I want my mommy!"'

Angel You gettin' along better with your mother?

Comet *looks at her.*

Angel Leavin' her to babysit while you's in the hospital.

Comet Who else?

Malika She give you that big birthday party ain't that a new thing? Generosity?

Comet Mother a the year.

Angel She was . . . Your mother . . . while you was in the hospital, all by herself she was babysittin' –

Comet First bruise I'da found on my baby I'da killed that bitch. And she knew I was serious cuz when I come home first thing I inspect my daughter head to toe. Knew I meant it. Not even diaper rash. (*Pause.*) Angel. Show me?

Malika   You ain't got it *yet*?

Angel *falls back on the bed laughing.*

Aintchu practised?

Comet   Practise all the time! just . . . if I see her do it once more . . . Angel?

Angel (*enjoying it*)   I dunno.

Comet   Come on.

Malika   Please Please Please Please!

Comet   I didn't say that! I just . . . (*She pulls a razor blade from her pocket.*) If I watch just one more time –

Angel   Okay.

Angel *takes the blade from* **Comet**, *puts it in her own mouth, twirls it around her mouth expertly, periodically flicking it on her tongue. Eventually takes it out, hands it back to* **Comet**.

Comet   God, I ain't never gonna be that good!

Malika   I can do it. Watch. (*Reaches for the razor.*)

Comet (*to* **Angel**)   I lost so much blood tryin' it, I do it in fronta the bathroom mirror.

Angel   I lost blood too, at first. Your tongue gotta develop a crust.

Malika   You gotta keep practisin'. J.W. says I'm totally sexy when I do it, watch. (*Reaches for the razor.*)

Comet (*to* **Angel**)   Practise any more I won't have a drop left. Watch.

Prix (*not looking up*)   I find a spot a blood on my floor the owner's gonna lose six pints more.

Comet, *who had started to put the blade into her mouth, doesn't. Offstage voices:*

Jerome   What did you say?!

Mother   I didn't say nothin'! I didn't say nothin'!

A bang, as if someone had been thrown against the wall. **Prix** *doesn't look up. A beat after the bang, then she speaks.*

Prix   Yaw stayin' all night?

Angel *and* **Malika** *get up* (**Comet** *was never sitting*).

Prix   Don't be late, Malika.

Malika   Why you always sayin' me? I guess Angel ain't never been late, why you gotta – ?

Prix   Don't be late, Malika.

Comet *is looking at* **Malika** *and* **Angel**.

Angel   Drive-by. McDonald's. 10:35.

Malika   You don't have to worry about me I'm starved. I'll bring J.W. for a bite 10 o'clock, by 10:35 I figure I be lip-smackin' Big Mac juice.

Prix   Comet, stay.

Malika *and* **Angel** *exit.* **Prix** *still hasn't looked up from her activity.* **Comet** *observes the room.*

Comet (*looking around*)   You sure like the fireworks.

Prix   Everybody likes the fireworks.

Offstage: a few moments' of laughter and sexual breathing, which irritates **Prix**. *After it quiets*:

Prix   'I'm gonna be eighteen, they catch me doin' what I'm doin' when I'm eighteen they put me away for life I'm quittin'! I'm quittin' the gang When my birthday comes I'm gone! Ain't a damn thing they can do about it!' I be eighteen myself two years and liar if I say it ain't crost my own mind, ain't a dumb idea. Mouthin' off about it was. Ways you coulda fucked up, got yourself thrown out. We'da kicked your ass and give ya the big punishment: you're gone. Now, stupid, gotcher ass kicked and here's the big punishment: you stay.

Prix *goes back to her pipe-cleaner figures. Quiet a few moments.*
Comet *mumbles something, then glances at* **Prix**, *waiting for* **Prix**
to ask her to repeat. **Prix** *doesn't.*

Comet   I *said*, I thought we ain't s'posed to hit on our
own, thought we only s'posed to spill blood a enemies. Or
strangers.

Prix (*dry*)   Yeah, we ain't s'posed to. See how low you
brung us. (*Beat.*) Dontchu know better than to walk into a
deserted narrow place, your sisters jus' waitin' for ya?

Quiet again.

Comet   Whatchu wanna do? Shoot 'em off?

Prix   Design 'em. (*Works quietly. Then.*) *And* shoot 'em off.
Fireworks people ain't a architect, make the blueprint and
give to someone else to build. Clothes designer never touch
a sewin' machine. A fireworks artist, take your basic
chrysanthemum, not to be confused with peonies, the latter
comprised a dots but chrysanthemums with petal tails, the
big flower start with a pistil of orange then move out into
blue, blue which comes from copper or chlorine, cool blue
burstin' out from orange pistil, blue instantly change to
strontium nitrate red to sodium yellow, cool to warm,
warmer and the designer ain't the joyful bystander, she's
right there pushin' the buttons and while the crowd's oohin'
aahin' this'n she's already on to the next button. This quick
chrysanthemum I'd start my show with and accompanying
reports of course, bang bang and I'll throw in a few willows,
slower timin' and a softer feelin', tension to relaxation keep
the audience excited, anticipatin', then time for multiple-
breakers, shell breakin' into a flower breakin' 'to another
flower 'to another, then a few comets (*Points to drawing on the
wall.*) Comets! Then, *then* if I had a bridge, a *Niagara*, fallin'
from the edge and this wouldn't even be the finale, maybe
. . . maybe . . . somethin' gooey, like 'Happy Birthday
Comet!' *Now* finale, which of course is the bombs and the
bombs and the bombs and 'chaos' can't possibly be the
description cuz this be the most precisely planned chaos you

ever saw! *Hanabi!* flowers of fire. My show people screamin'
it, '*Hanabi! Hanabi!*'

Offstage voices:

Jerome Bitch, where is it? (*Slap.*)

Mother I ain't got it!

Jerome You think I'm stupid?

Mother (*mocking*) 'You think I'm stupid?'

A brief struggle with furniture banging. **Comet** *continues admiring
the fireworks art.* **Prix**, *vaguely embarrassed by her preceding
enthusiasm, turns back to her project.*

Comet Sounds like my parents.

Prix He ain't my father.

The offstage noise quiets.

Prix (*not looking up*) This stuff gimme a sensa shape. But
sometimes I need the fire.

Prix *turns on her desk lamp, switches off the overhead lights. Pulls
several pen lights out of her drawer, clicks them on. The bulbs are
different colors. She begins moving them around, making different
fireworks shapes and sounds.* **Comet** *smiles. Suddenly big offstage
banging and arguing, screaming.*

Comet This fireworks finale I know too well. 'Bye. (*Exits.*)

Prix *goes back to her work. The battle rages on. A huge crash, then
silence.* **Prix** *continues working. Eventually*:

Mother (*outside door*) Prix?

No answer. **Mother** *opens the door, letting herself in, and shuts it
behind her. She is bruised from the fight.* **Prix** *doesn't look up.*

Prix Lock it.

Mother *does.*

Prix (*dry*) Guess he didn't kill ya.

Mother *laughs nervously.*

Prix   You kill him?

Mother   No, no he's okay. That crash . . . I hardly hit him
I think he's mostly passed out. Wine. Lots and lots and lotsa
. . . (*Sudden defensiveness.*) You think I wanted it? I got the
restrainin' order! I got it, fourteen years! Fourteen years
dumb! Fourteen years I been puttin' up with it, finally I wise
up, restrainin' order, six months it been effect, how many
times he been here that six months? Seven! And I called the
police first four times, him bangin' the door down. Slow as
they is, and Jerome skilled with a paper clip, no problem he
pick the lock 'fore they come, *if* they come why bother?

Prix (*still not looking up*)   Didn't have to pick the lock
tonight.

Mother   He was outside when I come home, o*kay?* I
didn't want him to come in. We was talkin'. . . . Think I
wanted it? It gonna happen anyway, I know it, I know it
while I'm talkin' even though he ain't said it, I ain't said it,
gonna happen and if I . . . if I let it happen, don't fight it, it
don't go over so rough. If I enjoy it a little, don't feel so
much like he made me. (*Beat.*) I gotta get out. 'Fore he
wakes, you be okay, you ain't the one he's after. I'm gettin'
out. (*Beat.*) You wanna come?

Prix *doesn't answer.*

Mother   I'm goin', you be okay. (*Puts her hand on doorknob.*)

Mother   Keep the door locked.

*She unlocks door and starts to open. A toilet flush is heard. She panics,
shuts door, locks. Loud whisper.*

Prix!

Prix *ignores her.*

Mother   *Prix!*

Prix, *angry and glaring, turns to* **Mother**.

Mother (*indicates the closet.*)   Can I – ?

Jerome (*offstage*)   Hey!

Mother *rushes into closet, shuts door.*

Prix   Smart. (*Sloppily kicks a large furniture piece in front of the door, then noisily throws open her window and slams it shut. Sits back down at her work.*)

Jerome (*outside the door, jiggling doorknob*)   I hear you! Dontcha be hittin' the damn fire escape!

A clicking sound in the doorknob. Then **Jerome** *forces the door open against the furniture and enters. Immediately rushes to the window, throws it open and steps out. A few moments later he returns, shutting the window behind him. He also looks roughed up from the fight with* **Mother**. **Prix** *continues her activity, not looking at him.*

Jerome (*playing with his paper clip*)   Whadju do, push her out?

Prix *doesn't look up.*

Jerome   Didn't notice her broken body writhin' on the ground so guess not. (**Jerome** *moves toward* **Prix**.) Wonder what we do 'til your mama get back.

Jerome *touches* **Prix** *sensually. At the first contact,* **Prix** *slams him against the closet door, surprising him, hurting him.*

Prix   I ain't five no more.

Prix *goes back to sit with her pipe cleaners, her back to him. Stunned,* **Jerome** *moves toward the door and exits. The outside door to the apartment opening and slamming shut. A few seconds of quiet, then the closet door is cracked open. Quiet weeping from inside. Eventually:*

Prix   If you weren't always playin' Helen Keller, bitch, you mighta knowed a long time ago.

The quiet weeping continues.

Scene Three

Institutional waiting room.

Angel *sits glue-sticking newspaper clippings into a scrapbook.* **Prix**
enters. She is startled to see **Angel**. **Angel** *sees* **Prix**.

Angel   Whatchu doin' here?

Prix *continues staring at* **Angel**. *As* **Angel** *chatters she continues
working on her scrapbook.*

Angel   Oh that's right, you got a mother in, since no one
but me and my mother ever visited her I forgot. Ain't seein'
her today though, Ramey *and* Sonia in Fuckers! I come all
the way out here LOCKDOWN! And Ramey's section's the
lockdownest, by the time they let him go visitin' time's
almost over. *And* all he wants to do five minutes we got is
bitch bitch bitch, jail sucks, no shit? But how 'bout just one
'Nice to see ya' to his girlfriend trekked all the way out here,
hour and a half subway and bus, think he appreciate that.
And I tell him too, then he wants to get pissed, *I* ain't
understandin', shit. If the dumbass hadn't been hangin' with
Carl I *told* him 'at greedy punk get him in trouble one day!
Three outa four cash registers they cleared and the idiot
waitin' around cuz Carl can't bear to leave the fourth
untouched. While he's clearin' it, guess what? (*Makes a siren
sound.*)

Prix   This ain't the men's side.

Angel   Seein' my sister, toldja Sonia in too.

Prix *glances at* **Angel**'*s book.*

Angel   Scrapbook. Thought Sonia like to see it. Was
gonna show it to Ramey 'til he pissed me off. Wanna see it?

Prix *shakes her head no.*

Angel (*looks at her*)   Your P.O. make you come?

Prix *nods.*

Angel   Glad I ain't been caught yet, no Probation Officer slave-masterin' my life. Better go in, time's runnin' out. She know?

Prix   P.O. told her. Probably just so P.O. can check on me after, see if I really done it.

Angel   Better go. Time's runnin' out.

Prix   What about you?

Angel   Forty-five minutes 'til they bring out the adolescents. But adult hour's now. She probably already there waitin' for ya. Go.

Beat.

Prix   You doin' that job? tomorrow?

Angel   Nope, takin' the day off.

Prix   Off?

Angel *looks at her.*

Maybe you ain't got that choice, Angel –

Angel *indicates her watch.* **Prix** *reluctantly enters another space where* **Mother***, who has been looking for* **Prix***, sits at a table with a small partition that separates* **Mother** *from the other side. The partition comes about as high as the neck of a sitting adult. A Corrections Officer (C.O.) stands nearby.* **Prix** *enters.* **Mother** *sees her, smiles broad but nervous, not knowing what to say.* **Prix** *doesn't move momentarily, a decision: then walks over and flops down in the chair opposite* **Mother***.* **Prix***'s body is turned to the side, away from* **Mother***, and she does not look at her.*

Mother   Surprise! They told me you was here but I didn't believe 'em. You look . . . You been eatin' right? Aunt BiBi tole me you been eatin' okay, I ast her to check on you now and again, she been by, right? (*No answer. Singsong teasing a small child.*) I know what tomorrow is. (*No answer. Little more nervous.*) And your birthday next month, I ain't forgot nunna them holidays, I made somethin' for ya. (*Pulls them out.* **Prix**

doesn't look.) Gloves! Hard to crochet 'em but . . . hope they fit . . .

Mother *reaches for* **Prix**'s *hand.* **C.O.** *makes a loud, surprised grunt and snatches the gloves.*

Mother   Sorry! Sorry! You can check 'em before you give 'em to her. Her birthday comin' up, 17. (*To* **Prix**.) Took me nine weeks to do it. Just learnin'.

C.O., *who has inspected the gloves, holds them out to* **Prix**. **Prix**, *who hasn't budged a muscle or her gaze, does not look at* **C.O.** **C.O.** *shakes the gloves to get* **Prix**'s *attention.* **Prix** *ignores* **C.O.** **C.O.** *lets gloves drop to the floor.*

Mother   When . . . When I get home I'm takin' you to Wave Hill. You never believed me, you think our neighborhood is all the Bronx is, uh uh. Bronx ain't just projects and bullets, there's parts got flowers, butterflies. Wave Hill, the Botanic Gardens. The Mansion in the Park! When I get home, first thing we do is go to the pretty things, no! No, 34th Street, twelve midnight. You never believed me 'bout that neither, toldja midnight, Empire State Building, lights out . . .

Toward the end of **Mother**'s *speech* **Prix**, *without warning, has got up and exited, back to the waiting room.* **Prix** *sits in a seat near* **Angel**. **Angel** *still glue-sticking.*

Angel (*not looking up*)   How'd it go? (*No answer.* **Angel** *doesn't notice.*) Wanna see my scrapbook?

Angel *opens the scrapbook.* **Prix** *pays scant attention. The book is filled with newspaper clippings.*

Angel (*pointing to various clippings*)   You remember Jeff Pace? Seventh grade, he made that environmental poster with the seals, won the contest? We was pretty good friends, I went to his funeral. Jeanine, remember? Too flirty. I knew she'd end up gettin' it cuz her homeboys always settin' her up to whore-spy on the enemy. She specifically requested her sexy pink dress, I know cuz she borrowed a piece a my notebook paper in U.S. history for her will, and here her mother laid her out like Sunday School. Tony, my ex. You went to his funeral, right? (*Dancing a brief fast dance.*) His had the best music. Oh! this whole spread, centerfold *and* next eight pages, all my big brother, all Vince. His football stuff, honor roll stuff. 'Athlete honor student killed by stray bullet.' That's Terri, Trish's little sister. She was eight, she got it in the head, hopscotchin' when a drive-by come flyin' through, remember? Here's Lenny –

Prix   You comin' tomorrow?

Angel   Pick your ears, Prix, I said no.

Prix *gets up to leave.*

Angel   Who the hell workin' tomorrow? Everybody want the day off.

Prix *heading for the door.*

Angel   You comin' to dinner?

Prix (*stops*)   Toldja I got a job to do. Somebody got to.

Angel (*shrugs*)   My mother told me to ask you. (*Pause.*) Wonder how come she up and did it. Your moms. You know?

Prix doesn't answer.

Angel   Coulda done him in years ago. Why now? (*Beat.*) First degree. Betcha: twenty-five to life. (*Beat.*) You was two when she met him, right? And he with yaw all them years, you miss him?

Prix   He wasn't my father.

Angel   My mom's gonna wonder why you ain't comin' to dinner, all alone tomorrow. Whatchu gonna eat?

Prix   Egg rolls. Like every other night.

Angel   Okay, Prix. (*Her face back in her scrapbook.*) Merry Christmas.

Prix *exits.* **Angel** *turns the pages of her scrapbook one by one, absorbed and content.*

Scene Four

Jail cell.

Bunk cots. By the lower bunk, a couple of new fireworks drawings. A chair. **Prix** *and* **Cat** *in street clothes,* **Cat** *with a cloth band around her hair.* **Prix***, in the chair, tears a page from a notebook she has just written on, stands to read.* **Cat** *listens.*

Prix   Six months ago a sense of personal injustice would have had me reaching for the trigger. Today I find my greatest defense is in open dialogue. It is the accepting, non-judgmental atmosphere of my counseling group that has allowed me to re-evaluate the choices I've made. Your support has opened me to revisit my mistakes and has helped me to see my errors as attributable to social and economic circumstances of my upbringing as well as to personal choice. My home was violent, my teachers suspicious, potential employers uninterested. Sometimes I think if I had been shown one kindness in my life, perhaps things could have been different. While I am naturally apprehensive about the consequential changes our group will undergo, I celebrate the release of three of you over the next several days, and welcome those newcomers who will be filling your seats. On this last day that we are one, my sisters, I joyously thank you for replenishing my soul and touching my heart.

She has read seriously and continues silently looking at the page a few moments. Suddenly no longer able to contain it, she bursts into uncontrollable laughter. **Cat** *follows suit.*

Cat   'My sisters', 'My sisters'!

Prix*'s laughter subsides. She sits, erases on the paper, edits.*

Cat (*no pause from previous speech*)   That's funny, you're smart. They eat up that crap, how long it take 'em figure it's shit? I like to see the look on their faces, I'm comin' to your group tomorrow.

Prix (*not looking up*)   You ain't in my group.

Somewhere in **Cat**'s *following speech,* **Prix** *pulls out from under her cot a box of colored pencils and starts sketching. Will not look up.*

Cat   I am now. I told Miss Collins I didn't feel comfortable in my group, she said Give it a try, you only been here a month, I said Some of them bitches threatenin' me, say they gonna take my teeth out. Randy. Scooter. She said I'll talk to 'em. I said I wish you wouldn't. That really make life hell, I wish you just change my group please. The lie is, Randy and Scooter never said nothin' 'bout my teeth, I just hate their ugly faces wanted get away from 'em. The truth is, Miss Collins tell 'em what I said I *would* be in life-threatenin' trouble for lyin' 'bout 'em the first place. Luckily Miss Collins buy it I'm your group tomorrow. I like your group I like them people. (*Pause.*) Lap a luxury. Three meals. Street clothes.

Prix   You the only one around here ready to print up the welcome travelers' brochure for jail.

During **Cat**'s *following speech,* **Jerome** *will enter the cell, walking across the stage.* **Prix** *will pull out her gun and shoot him dead. Then go back to her sketching. Eventually he will skootch off the opposite side of the stage.*

Cat   I hear 'em! Cryin' on the phone, 'My honey, my honey,' 'I miss my friends.' Most of 'em's honeys was kickin' the shit out of 'em daily and their *friends?* Their best girlfriend's on the outside and so's their honey guess what one plus one is equalin'? (*Beat.*) Could be worse. See them ugly green one-piece things they make the women wear? Least adolescents, we wear our own shit. (*Beat.*) Easy time. Five months you be eighteen, outa here, eleven left for me, shit. Scotfree both us and I'm fifteen, three more years a minor, I get caught, easy time. Eleven months I *know* my roof? *know* my mealtimes? shit. Damn sure beats the fosters.

Prix   Usually all I hear's you whinin' 'bout the clothes situation.

Cat   Lacka choices! I *love* my clothes, but wearin' the same
five outfits gets limitin' after awhile. There's this cute thing I
useta wear, black, kinda sheer, kinda spare, my belly button
on the open-air market. They say No way, Stupid! Their
Nazi dress code, what. They think wearin' it'll get me
pregnant? in *here*? (*Beat.*) Ain't my first time in. Fourth!

Prix   Runaway.

Cat   Three more years I'm a fuckin' criminal for it! can't
wait 'til eighteen! Runnin' away I be legal! (*Beat.*) My broken
arm was mindin' its own business wisht they'da minded
theirs, dontcha never believe that crap about best to tell the
counselor tell the teacher it'll makes things better. Cuz ya
will get sent back home and just when ya thought things
could get no worse, they do.

Prix   *Sh!*

Prix *moves against the wall. Someone is tapping against it, a code.*
Prix *taps back in code. When the communication is complete,* **Prix**
sits back down to her sketching. **Cat** *smiles.*

Cat   What's the big one? Single most thing earned you all
the gracious undivided esteem? I heard this: shot a enemy
girl in the face. Then went to her funeral cuz yaw was best
friends second grade, made all your sisters go, put the whole
goddamn family on edge and everyone one of 'em knew and
not a one of 'em said a word about it to you. (*Beat.*) *And* one
time jumpin' a girl in, she not too conscious, you jump your
whole weight on her face ten times maybe? twelve? 'fore a
sister pull you off. *And* when yaw stand around, eenie
meenie minie pick some herb comin' down the subway steps
to steal their wallet, you was the one everybody know could
always knock 'em out first punch. *And* one time on a revenge
spree, dress up like a man so no one identify you later, stick
your hair under a cap and shoot dead some boy ten years
old. *And* –

Prix   Fifteen.

Pause. **Cat** *is confused.*

Prix   I don't kill no kids. Fifteen.

Cat   O.G.! you gonna earn it. Original Gangsta, people
respect you long after you retire Take me in! (*No answer.*)
You get it. The high, right? This girl Aleea, she tell me all
about it. The kickin' and smashin' and breakin' bones snap!
Somebody lyin' still in a flood a their own blood, somebody
dead it gets her all hyped up, thrill thing! And power, them
dead you not, *you* made it happen! Them dead, *you* done it!
You ever get that high?

Prix   'Course.

During **Cat***'s following speech,* **Jerome** *will enter from the same
side of the stage from where he'd entered before, again walking across.*
Prix *takes* **Cat***'s hair band –* **Cat** *doesn't notice – and effortlessly
strangles* **Jerome** *to death.*

Cat   Take me in! I tried once, not yours. Not the other
neither I ain't enemy! Small little club I was interested in.
Wore the right colors, I talked the shit. They wouldn't even
jump me in, I said 'I'll do it! Either way, all yaw stand in a
line and rough me through it OR I'll take the toughest one
on, two minutes!' They just laugh. (*Beat.*) Maybe when we
out . . . I know there's lots and lots a members, big network
your group, maybe . . . I'd be good! Runnin' with my sisters,
tappin' the codes –

Prix (*strangling*)   Wannabe.

Prix *back to her sketching.* **Jerome** *eventually gets off the opposite
side of the stage, his mode of movement different from the last time.*

Cat   They think I ain't tough I got it! I can fight! I was
four, these two boys was six, tried to steal my bike I flattened
'em! And when my foster sisters steak-knife stabbed me and
drowned me in the tub, somebody called a ambulance, he
mouth-to-mouthed me back alive, said if I wasn't strong I'da
stayed dead. (*Chuckles.*) *She*'s dead! Jessie, she the one
screamin' 'Hold her down! No air bubbles hold the bitch 'til
she dead dead dead!' Look who's talkin', she with her
homegirls and -boys thinkin' she a member in good

standin', got drunk one night and said somethin' smart to a homey, he blew her head off. (*Laughs*.)

Prix   You ever wish you done it?

Cat (*Beat*)   Huh?

Prix   You ever . . . You ever regret wasn't you pulled that trigger?

Cat (*confused*)   She's dead.

Prix   Yeah but like . . . that thought. Fantasy. It ever get stuck your mind? Wishin' the last thing she seen was you robbin' her last breath?

Officer Dray (*offstage, yelling to someone else*)   You heard me, I said Move on!

Cat   Bitch! You know that ol' crackhead Tizzy? Officer Dray told me I was mouthin' off, I wa'n't doin' nothin'! She goes Move along and I do and she goes Don't roll your eyes at me! and I go I *moved* along and she goes Don't gimme nunna your lip! and I go (*'What're-you-yelling-at-me-for?' gesture*.) and she goes Alright goddammit mop the floor with Tizzy! and I think Oh fuck but I do it, shit. And ol' Tizzy don't shut up, bitchin' all outa her head, and I go Oh shut up ya ol' crackhead bitch! And she goes, (*suddenly struggling to contain laughter*) she goes, 'Hey! One day you gonna be me!'

Prix *looks up, not at* **Cat**. **Cat** *is rolling on her bed, uncontrollable laughter*.

Scene Five

Counseling room.

Fuego *and* **Shondra** *sit. The room is represented by four or five folding chairs, indicating that this is half of a larger circle of perhaps ten people.*

Shondra   What makes me mad? What makes me mad is the shit they call food. Allow us no chocolate but meanwhile what *is* that cold fried shit they slop on our plates? Tater tots? What the shit is tater tots? What makes me mad is goddamn body searches before visits, after visits. What makes me goddamn mad is havin' to sit here talkin' shit and listen to all you talkin' shit when I don't give a goddamn and you don't give a goddamn, that's what makes me mad.

Cat *enters.*

Fuego (*indicating the 'counselor'*)   I think she means what makes us mad on the outside.

Cat   Hi, Fuego. Hi, Shondra. (*Sits.*)

Shondra (*eyes on 'Counselor'*)   Hi. I *told*ju in individual counselin' why the shit I gotta be dredgin' up my business in fronta everybody.

Feugo   So we can help each other. (*Breaks into laughter.*)

Cat   Missin' classes when there's a lockdown, that's what makes me mad.

Fuego   Fuck ain't nunna these bitches I look to for help 'less I need help gettin' my throat slashed, there I find lotsa helpful friends.

Shondra   I got no friends. I got sisters. And associates.

Cat   The clothes make me mad. How come only five outfits?

Shondra (*to* **Cat**)   I catch you lookin' at my stuff in the shower again I'ma mess you up.

Cat   I wa'n't lookin' at you!

Shondra (*to 'Counselor'*)   Don't tell *me* this ain't the place for that! I see some bitch lookin' between my legs I'ma –

Cat (*mumbles*)   Like you two don't do it.

Fuego   Whadju say?

Shondra (*to* **Cat**)   Yeah, dontchu worry about it.

Fuego (*to* **Cat**)   Whadju say?

Shondra   She said she was fuckin' lookin' where it was nunna her uglyass business to be lookin'.

Cat   I saw . . . I saw . . .

Shondra   Stupid obviously don't understand the difference, wants and needs. I *need* a man's touch but none around, I take what I can get. But if you *look*in', Tom-peepin', that's cuz you *wan*nit, you *want* a woman and you was probably doin' women out there

Cat   I wasn't!

Shondra (*uninterrupted*)   And tell ya somethin' else,

Cat I wasn't doin' it! (*Beat.*) I WON'T DO IT NO MORE!	**Shondra** this be your one warnin'. I ever catch you –

Prix *enters and sits. At first sight of her,* **Shondra** *and* **Fuego** *sit up straight, fall to silence. They don't look at her, or at each other.* **Cat** *had continued speaking until becoming aware of the sudden stillness. She is surprised by the fear-respect. Takes it in. Suddenly* **Cat**'s *head turns, as if called on by the counselor.*

Cat   Home? Mmmmm . . . I guess . . . the garbage. Makes me mad when the garbage gets piled high my street, the rats . . . It ain't even a strike! If it was a strike I'd understand but regular thing, that high garbage, these rats –

Fuego   I don't understand the damn system, I don't see how I can get charged nine felonies when they only caught me doin' two. (*New thought, looks at the Counselor.*) They gotta prove it. (*Waits momentarily for an answer; when none comes.*) They gotta prove it! right?

Shondra   Not respectin'. Cuz I been doin' it a long time, I got some experience. Then somebody, fourteen, fuck up the goddamn instructions, I get on her about it, she say, 'I didn't forget the codes.' I get on her about it, slam her head

'gainst the cement wall, 'I didn't forget the codes.' I slam it
slam it slam it, 'I didn't forget the codes.' Last thing I hear
some kinda mumble, 'I didn't – ' lyin' to the end out on the
ground, out cold I kick her stupid stubborn face. All she had
to do was admit it, shit. And if I'd killed the dumb bitch,
guess *I*'d be the bad guy.

A silence.

Fuego   My sister Enrica, she taught me Backgammon,
she's fifteen, I'm nine, we're still in Texas. Every time she
roll double sixes, she go, 'Boxcars! Boxcars! Lucky!' Then,
one day Enrica suddenly all mean, screamin' all over the
house, *loca!* And this bad mood don't pass. Hear me rollin'
the backgammon dice, she come punchin' my face, Mami
have to pull her off. Monday at school the girls giggle at me,
'*Hermana* boxcar! *Hermana* boxcar!' Eventually tell me Enrica
joined the gang, attached to a boy gang and new girls gotta
roll in. They hand Enrica two dice. Boxcars, but this game
boxcars is bad luck. Twelve of 'em. Toughest boy was
engine. Littlest boy caboose. (*Beat.*) I like New York better. I
like jumpin' in here, better 'n rollin' in, all I got from
jumpin' in was a couple broken ribs they healed.

Silence.

Cat (*suddenly sobbing*)   They took 'em away! They took 'em
away!

Shondra   *What?*

Cat   Little boy!

Fuego   What're you talkin' about?

Cat   Had a baby! Little boy, they make me, they make me
adopt him away!

Fuego   Can't no one make ya ya musta said yes.

Cat   They said do it! They said Do it!

Shondra   Where was ya gonna put him? Get a double
cell, one be the nursery?

Cat   Before I was charged! I oughtn't be here no way, awaitin' trial, innocent 'til proven guilty, how come I gotta sit here for lacka five hundred?

Fuego   *Five hundred?*

Cat looks at her.

Fuego   *Dollars?*

Cat *nods, confused.*

Fuego   Not five hundred thousand.

Cat   No!

Fuego   Fuck I wish *my* bond was fuckin' five hundred dollars, I'm here 'til I come up with ten thousand here to eternity.

Shondra   Depends on whatchu in for. Whatchu in for?

Shondra *knows.* **Cat**, *caught, scared, refuses to answer.*

Shondra   Well let's see what could possibly be judged that puny bail.

Shondra *looking at* **Fuego**. **Fuego** *confused a moment, then gets it.*

Fuego   *Prostitution?*

Cat   They ain't proved nothin' yet!

Fuego   *Prostitution?*

Cat   FUCK YOU! like you any better!

Fuego   *Hell*uva lot better I ain't never taken no money for it I ain't never been *that*.

Shondra   If ya took it for money you be a – (*to 'counselor'.*) No, I *won't* shut up! If ya took it for money maybe ya still have a little dignity. Funky filthy on the street, whore been tradin' it for a Big Mac.

Fuego *roars with laughter.*

Cat   AIN'T TRUE!

Shondra   Is and you know it, I know somebody goddamn bought the burger. (*To 'counselor'.*) *What?*

Cat   You'da done it too! you was hungry! You was hungry like I was –

Fuego   I don't get that hungry.

Cat   You don't know!

Shondra and **Fuego** *laughing hard.*

Cat   FUCK YOU! YOU DON'T KNOW!

Shondra and **Fuego** *doubled over laughing.* **Cat** *turns her back away from them and from the audience. Freeze.* **Prix**, *who's silently enjoyed the fight, speaks.*

Prix (*in her head*)   What makes me mad is music. John Philip Souza, trombone pansy crap. And I *tried* Boulez, shit he *wrote* for 'em but most of it's too damn obvious. Still, I go for the *1812* cliché. And my head's designed about seven rap shows, comets for the basic beat, butterflies and palm trees the chorus. Chrysanthemums ain't on any regular rhythm but rather hit the hardcore politicals: 'power' and 'fight' and 'black black black'! But it's all stupid, first of all the differential between speed a sound and speed a light means music and visuals ain't never be lined up perfect like some goddamn video, and who *needs* it? Fireworks got their own music: reports and hummers, whistles. Magic, each one born with that little sound. A gulp. A breath. And we holdin' *our* breaths, waitin' (*Soft.*) three . . . four . . . five . . . BOOM! And my *heart* boom boomin', the final moment of the finale bang! flash! (*Beat.*) Then nothin' left but pastel smoke, pink, blue floatin' calm. Calm.

Scene Six

Cell.

As **Cat** *chatters she will pull the sheet off the upper bunk, then sit tying it. She is cheery.* **Prix** *reads a tattered paperback black romance novel, does not look at* **Cat**.

Cat (*admiration*)   You the coldest fish I know! Ruthless! People know it too, you walk into a room, silence! (*New idea.*) Prix. Come to my geometry tomorrow. I like geometry but those dumb bitches just come in bitchin', bitchin' interrupt the class then I don't learn nothin' but you walk in, everybody shut up, everybody know who you are, get quiet fast, come on, geometry! I like that math. Circles is three sixty, a line goes on and on, rectangle versus the parallelogram, interestin'! Ain't fireworks geometry? Can't the study a angles and arcs be nothin' but helpful? Come on! Favor for me?

Prix *chuckles to herself.* **Cat**, *not necessarily expecting the refusal, is delighted by it.*

Cat   I know! you don't do favors! You the coldest fish I know! (*Beat.*) You met Ms Bramer? She's the new Current Events. She's nice I hope she stick around awhile. She say the 6 o'clock news always hypin': 'Tough on teens! Youth violence outa hand, try 'em like adults!' But she say news never say three times as many murders committed by late 40s as by under-18s, news never say for every one violence committed by a under-18, *three* violences committed by adults *to* under-18s, if we violent where we learn it? Sow what you reap.

Prix   Reap what you sow.

Cat (*having just noticed* **Prix**'s *reading material*)   I know that book! passed to me months ago. She's a lawyer, pro bono, he's a big record producer. He's rich and she appreciates it but she don't know, loooves him but got that lawyer's degree and don't know she can lower herself to *that*. I didn't

think you read that stuff, I love you and roses and wet eyes.
(*Beat.*) You ever plan your funeral?

Prix   Fireworks.

Cat   Knew it! Nothin' somber for me neither, I got the
tunes all picked out, went through my CD collection I know
who my special guest stars be, I figure they come, like this
poor unfortunate 15-year-old girl died, ain't the city violent
and sad? We feel so depressed we come give a free funeral
concert, her last request. Good publicity for them. Here's
the processional tune: (*She begins humming a lively hip hop piece.
Interrupts herself.*) Processional, when the people first walks in
with the casket. (*Resumes her humming. Stops.*) My coffin's
gonna be open. Yours?

Prix *turns a page.*

Cat   I'm gonna look good, I got the dress picked and I
want people to see it. You ever plan your suicide?

Prix   Fifth grade.

Cat   Pills? Gun stuck up your mouth?

Prix   Off the Brooklyn Bridge. (*Now puzzled.*) Would that
kill ya?

Cat   World Trade Center better bet, know how many
freefall floors to concrete? Hundred ten!

Prix   Knew this girl, Emmarine. Eighth grade social
studies. Her thirteenth birthday tried, fucked it up. Now she
got little cuts on her wrists and everyone at school smirkin'
wherever she walks. On her locker, someone spray-paint
'Emmarine, Suicide Queen', like they ain't never thought of
it themself, and someone else ex out 'Queen', write over it
'Flop.'

Cat   You noticed I ain't been around last twenty-four?
Infirmary, doctor checkin' me out after this girl come up to
me *pow!* She say, 'What your name?' I'm tryin' to answer,

'My name's Cat' but before I get the first word out *pow!* She punch me in my face I'm all knocked out!

Prix   Not any damn home sets I'm gettin' professional stuff, Class B pyrotechnics, the flowers and 'falls and rain takin' up the whole sky, in my will the details of this spectacular will be specified, my careful plannin' will reap the benefits: the audience mesmerizement, the big boom!

Cat   Supper tonight, I seen her people, them girls follows her around, she weren't there guess they threw her in the bean. I come to her girls, say, 'Your friend ask me what my name is. My name's Cat.' But soon as I say 'Your friend ask me what my name is' they start laughin' so hard I think they don't hear the second part, so I keep sayin' it louder but the louder I say it the louder they laugh. '*My name is Cat!*' (Giggles.) 'MY NAME IS CAT!' (*Giggles, stands on the upper bunk.*)

Prix   Most appropriate funeral finale cuz they wasn't just my life. My death. Tragic, someone gimme cotton socks, I *think*, Christmas present and I walk into the workshop wearin' 'em. 'Cep' turns out they was silk. Static electricity, spark, boom! 'God,' they say, 'how could this happen? To *her*? Always double-checkin' her clothing, she of all people.' Scene a the unfortunate event, they note how I generously spaced apart each of my twenty-five little fireworks houses so one accident is prevented from causin' a chain reaction and they'll wipe their wet cheeks, touched that I protected others, touched I died alone. So young, so young.

As **Prix** *spoke,* **Cat** *had swung the sheet (which she'd tied into a rope) around an overhead horizontal pipe and secured it. It is suddenly clear that she has formed a noose. Standing on the edge of the bunk, she has stuck her head through it. If she jumps off, she'll hang. The cheeriness has vanished. her eyes are closed, her breathing harsh and uneven. The most delicate push would be enough to knock her over. Now* **Prix** *turns to* **Cat***, looking at her for the first time in the scene. Though* **Prix** *had not been aware of* **Cat***'s activity, she does not look surprised.*

Prix   Jump.

Act two

Scene One

Kitchen table.

Prix *and* **Jerome** *at opposite sides, he sipping coffee, she with a fast-food milkshake. On the table are a clock-radio, a gun, and many vials of crack which* **Prix** *silently counts, moving her lips. She will periodically glance at the time.*

Jerome   Way I figure it, woulda made better sense I killed her. Statistically speaking, man kill his wife, whether from a argument whether he stalked her, crime a passion, three, four years tops. Woman kill her husband, response to him whoopin' the devil outa her decade or two, it's murder one, she get twenty-five to life. Seven years since she gimme the gun, she ain't yet served a third a the minimum time. Other way 'round, I'da been out, parta regular life four years now in the simple name a freedom, in the name a quality a human life, wouldn't me snuffin' her been the more logical choice, long run?

Prix   You weren't her husband.

Jerome   Common law. Fourteen years we was together, common law husband –

Prix   Shut up! you're mixin' me up.

Jerome   And common law father to you, man whose genes you got you never met. If your mama even know who that is so I'm the only father you ever . . . (**Prix** *is looking at him.*) Okay! I wasn't the best daddy Who's perfect? Only said I was all the daddy you had. Maybe I wasn't around for *conception*, maybe I didn't *breathe* life into ya not there glimpse your first breath, but I was around pretty much all the breaths thereafter I think I had a impact, your life. Sometimes . . . Sometimes your mama couldn't make the rent, I help her out a little. Once I remember her flat broke, I bought the shoes for ya.

Prix (*flat*)   I don't remember that.

Jerome   Seven years old tap-dancin' the shoe store, new white buckle sandals.

Prix   You lied your whole life now guess you gonna lie your whole death.

Jerome   I gave yaw money! I remember . . . I remember helpin' with the groceries once –

Prix   Shut up!

Beat. **Jerome** *picks up the gun, studies it.*

Jerome   Your mama always found it such a curiosity, fireworks fixation. All make sense to me, one way or another you love the bang bangs.

Prix   Chinese invention, they find a purpose: beautiful. Spiritual. Not 'til a English monk put his two cents in do white people decide gunpowder for killin'. (*The noisy end of the milkshake.*)

Jerome   Ain't that a healthy breakfast, chocolate shake. Hey. Thought you had to go out, big appointment.

Prix   Gotta do the inventory some point. Long as I'm waitin' – (*Eyes on clock-radio.*) When the fuck – ?

Jerome   If you was smart you'da put your time inside to some kinda trainin', no need it have to be total waste but no. Your brain too much the street.

Prix   Since they recently slashed the higher ed, I'm left with these options: specialize in shampoo, specialize in relaxers. I say I liketa specialize in Class B pyrotechnics. They say ha ha, real likely they apprenticeship a felon with explosives.

Jerome   Boo hoo life so hard. Least you had counselin', school. I got nothin', dropped out and into the army, pulled in by the college promise, then they fine-print robbed me out of it. And the kinda job trainin' I got be real useful. Next time some country invade New York. Think I sit around woe-is-me? Always found somethin', *legal*. Street cleanin', janitor –

Phone rings.

Jerome   One time –

Prix *makes a brief shush noise-gesture, glaring at him. Phone rings a second time, third. At the first sound of the fourth, she picks up. Lets the other person speak first.*

Prix   Oh, you.

Jerome   Maybe I wa'n't Daddy a the Year but I offered support, legal.

Prix (*into receiver*)   I was hopin' it was them, you're late. Come up, I gotta go.

Jerome   What, you think you be up for the complementary daughter award? You sure ain't the gran' prize! Your own mama, seven years and you ain't writ, ain't seen her, not since that probation officer enforce ya, sixteen.

Prix   I ain't got time, Comet.

Jerome   But then how couldja visit. Never bothered find out what prison she been moved to. Five years back.

Prix *hangs up, obviously cutting off* **Comet**. *Puts on jacket, takes gun back, pulls from jacket pocket a little notepad, studies.*

Jerome   You ain't got that intercom fixed yet? All this time, still somebody gotta announce theyselves by the cross-the-street pay phone? Then you guess how long it take 'em get back across, buzz 'em in.

Prix, *paying no attention to* **Jerome**, *pushes the buzzer and holds it a few seconds.*

Jerome   Lucky. So far. You ain't been to jail since that year in juvie, and your auntie move into your apartment, bigger 'n hers, hold it for ya 'til ya get back. Be there when ya get out, family company. But, released, your damn attitude drive her out after four months, get caught your business this time you be put away *years*, and who you think hold on to your home this time? No one! Gone! (*Knock at the door.*) Ain't twenty-four bit old still be playin' gang gal?

Prix *glances through the door peephole, begins undoing the various door locks.*

Jerome   You goin' back. Lucky, you been kickin' all six years since you got outa teen hall and your blind parole police ain't suspected a thing, but sometime you goin' down, I got a prediction for your life: jail – second home.

Prix, *who's finished unlocking, relatches a lock.*

Comet   PRIX! (*Pounding.*)

Jerome   No, first.

Prix   WAIT!

Pounding stops. **Prix** *walks to a closet.*

Prix   Here's a present.

Prix *takes out of the closet a cupcake with a candle that is obviously a stick of dynamite.*

Jerome (*pleased*)   You remembered.

Prix   I better let her in 'fore she breaks it down. You light the candle later.

Jerome *smiles and exits off the side of the stage opposite the outside door, which* **Prix** *opens. During* **Comet**'s *following speech, the sudden reflection of various colored lights – fireworks – from the direction* **Jerome** *exited.* **Prix** *notices without expression.* **Comet** *doesn't notice.*

Comet (*drops into a kitchen chair*)   Jesus givin' me all that shit for bein' late then take ten minutes to open the goddamn door! And I *told*ju in the first place I might be five minutes delayed cuz my mother gotta come watch the baby I *do* have kids you know.

Prix   I needja to answer the phone.

Comet   You called me over here for that? When you gettin' a fuckin' cell phone, Prix?

Prix, *looking over her notes, ignores* **Comet**.

Comet   Why me?

Prix   Cuz you on the payroll.

Comet   Call me all the way over here –

Prix   They left a message on the machine, I better be here 11 to 11:30 cuz they be callin', they leave no number for me to call back. Meanwhile I have another appointment, pickup I gotta do now.

As **Comet** *speaks,* **Prix** *pulls a backpack out of the closet, starts emptying it.*

Comet   So fuckin' sicka this. Thought kids I'd give up the life. Welfare sure don't cut it. I gotta gangbang supplemental income for the luxuries: food. Diapers.

Prix   Let it ring three times, *exactly three times*. The moment you hear the fourth ring start pick it up. Say nothin', they'll talk. Take notes. (*Tears relevant pages out, tosses rest of the pad to* **Comet**.) At the end they say 'Got it?' you say 'Got it.' And you *have* it. (*Stares at* **Comet**, *no response*.) O*kay?*

Comet   O*kay!*

Prix   I'll be back fast they may not even call by then. Right on the corner. Five minutes.

Prix *shuts the door behind her.* **Comet** *looks around, bored. Turns on the radio and searches 'til she finds a station she likes. Eventually the phone rings.* **Comet** *quickly turns off radio. Phone rings three times. Stops ringing.* **Comet** *is freaked, doesn't know what to do. Picks up receiver, quickly puts it back. Eventually phone begins ringing again. She is confused, panicked. As the third ring commences she snatches the receiver, listens. Gives a little cry.*

Comet   Shit! Shit! Shit! Shit! Shit!

She stares at the phone, crazy. **Prix** *enters, sets her backpack down.*

Prix   They call?

Comet *doesn't answer.* **Prix** *looks at* **Comet**.

Comet   THREE! rang three times and I was waitin' for
the fourth but it STOPPED! God it STOPPED and I was
scared I miscounted or they miscounted or they toldju
wrong then it started ringin' again GOD! God Oh Jesus I
thought Oh Jesus Should I pick up? should I – I did! I – I
guess I was afraid it would stop ringin' again so I guess I
picked it up picked it up too soon JESUS! Oh JESUS they
hung up! I picked it up JESUS I'm SORRY, Prix! Jesus they
hung up I'm sorry, Prix.

Prix, *seething, glares at* **Comet**. *Finally opens her mouth to speak
but before any words come out, the phone rings again. They both stare
at it. At the top of the fourth ring* **Prix** *snatches the receiver and the
pad.* **Comet**'s *entire body relieved.* **Prix** *jots down notes.*

Prix   Got it.

Hangs up. Sits in the other chair, not looking at **Comet**. *Thinking.
Quiet.*

Comet   Prix –

Prix   'Bye, Comet.

Comet *goes to the door. Opens it. Then suddenly turns to* **Prix**.

Comet   I ain't just nothin', Prix! Know that's whatchu
think soft, Soft Comet, still cries at movies still cries at
funerals, I don't want it! I never asked to be boss, Prix! You
act like I'm failin' at ambition, PRIX! I'M HERE! WHERE
I WANNA BE I never asked for nothin' but a little stash to
sell, just get me my kids by. I ain't got your leadership
quality, Prix, don't name me worthless just cuz my
personality don't got what yours does: the ice.

Comet *exits.* **Prix** *stares thoughtfully after* **Comet** *awhile, then
opens the bag and pulls out the new vials. Silently counts.*

Scene Two

Prison cell.

Prix *and* **Denise** *in prison uniforms.* **Denise** *putting sponge rollers in her hair.* **Prix** *lying supine on her upper bunk staring at the ceiling. A personal letter out of its envelope lies flat on her belly.*

Denise   Four years we been together, I assumin' you got nary a friend in the world. Then ha ha, joke on me: here come a letter. That the first you had since you been in, right? (*No answer.*) I seen the return. 'Nother prison. But can't be nothin' too excitin', no big deals bein' made cuz sure thing they tore 'at sucker open, read it, must be personal, I heard you's all alone in the world, who you got personal? (*No answer.*) How come you got no kids? How ol' you, twenty-eight? By the time I was twenty-eight I had six and pregnant with number seven. I heard 'boutchu. I know 'boutchu but the rumors conflict. You been with it all, men, women, dogs. Flip side: never been touched. Which? (*No answer.*) Come on! I got a cigarette bet on the former. Betchu lost your virginity early in the day, how ol'? thirteen? Twelve?

Prix (*dry*)   Five.

Denise   *Yes!* Terror terror. You was one of 'em, right? I done a little damage my day but you was a biggie I hear. Pre-18 but you knew when to stop. Get the hardcore felonies erased, your permanent record. You be out soon, three years, right? Three be gone 'fore ya know it. I ain't even be parole eligible for at least next five.

Prix   Two.

Denise *puzzled.*

Prix   My sentence was six. Served four years I be out two.

Denise   See! no time. My steady assignment was undercover, fool the white people, let the ATM people feel safe, thinkin' this white girl in with 'em. 'Just don't open your mouth, Paley,' what my girls call me, 'don't open your mouth 'til you pull the knife cuz soon's you part them pink lips your cover be blown: projects all over!' (*Guffaws.*)

Prix (*as* **Denise** *laughs*)   You *are* white.

Denise   How I be white, onliest white people I ever see is TV. Teachers. Fifth grade bus trip to the museum. Might be born white how I stay white no role models. (*Beat.*) I don't mean to be in your business but I couldn't help but notice the return: same last name.

Long pause.

Prix   Mother. Junkie. Started in jail I guess Never touched it when I knew her.

Denise   When you knew her?

Prix   Last time . . . sixteen.

Denise   You was *sixteen*? Ain't seen her *twelve years*? (*No answer.*) She wrote to tell you she's a junkie?

Prix   Wrote to tell me AIDS. Early release. Pro bono.

Denise (*pause*)   Not me. Not my kids, whatever happens . . . Every Tuesday I see 'em, once a month my mother, we stickin' it out, the family ties we –

Sudden teenage laughter, rowdiness, in the corridor. **Denise** *rushes to the bars to see. After they have passed and it is quiet again:*

Denise   I like the Ladies' groups. You like 'em? The counselin', classes. I missed my 8:30 readin' class this mornin' and sat in on the adolescents' 10 o'clock to make up. Rowdy! Forgot how rowdy they get, way *we* was SO glad not to be around that no more, so glad not to *be* that no more. Least Ladies got *some* kinda respect, 'preciate we know how to be: polite to each other, quiet to each other. With them two new ones now we got nine, nine's a good group.

Prix   Eight.

Denise   Aintchu precise with the numbers today! Too bad you weren't so quick when ya screwed up the codes yesterday breakfast.

Pause.

Prix   *What?*

Denise   I heard that girl servin' the slop take your tray, tap it three times, plop the scrambled eggs your plate, tap the tray seven times. Three, *seven.* Then I heardja pass by that other bitch and out the side a your mouth, 'Thirty-*eight.*'

Prix *stares at her.*

Prix   She tapped eight times!

Denise   I could see where you could make the mistake. She did somethin', took a little breath space between third and fourth taps and your mind accidentally filled in the extra.

Prix *stunned, confused. Then looks at* **Denise***, about to protest.*

Denise   Yeah. I'm sure.

Prix (*incredulous*)   She fucked me up. She fucked me up!

Denise   Ain't the first time this month neither. Messin' up, tell ya, I useta be in it but when my babies startin' comin', re*tire.* And gettin' into a fuckup habit's one sure sign you bess do the same.

Prix   Wait. That deal went down yesterday afternoon. I seen her yesterday evenin'. You're the one that's fucked up, if I'm screwed I'da sure knowed it by now.

Denise   You're screwed. I overheard. She just waitin' for the moment.

Prix   How do you know?

Denise *doesn't answer.* **Prix** *yanks* **Denise***'s head back.*

Prix   *How do you know?*

Denise   I just heard it! I ain't with noboby no more!

Prix *still holds* **Denise***'s head back a few moments, then lets go.*

Denise   That's the point. On the outside lookin' in, comfy chair. Sit back, watch the sparks fly without bein' one of 'em. From my viewpoint, I can predict it all.

Prix   She's gonna kill me, fuck.

Denise   Predicted you'd mess up. When I was in it, thirty-seven meant shipment pickup in the laundry room, thirty-eight the gym. Guess things changed by now?

Prix   She's gonna kill me! fuck!

Denise   You been in it too long, in it too long ya lose it. O.G. everybody want it. O.G. Original Gangsta, shit. You earned that years ago, what you stick around for? Ain't twenty-eight bit old for the gangs? (*Hair.*) I'm gonna cut all this shit off. My hair get curlier when it's close, and them close cuts all sophistication. (*Pause.*) When you said you was gonna make a fireworks show. You serious? (*No answer.*) I sure as hell couldn't. Set a thing up, then see one a them hot sparks fly off, come fallin' down right on top a ya *no!*

Pause.

Prix   Scariest is the opposite. Black shell. Send it up and somethin' go wrong: it don't explode. And in the blacka night, you can't see where it's fallin'. You know that live explosive's on the way back down, right down to ya. You just can't see where it's comin' from.

Scene Three

Denise *sits on a bench smoking, watching* **Socks** *push a broom.* **Denise***'s broom stands idle against the wall near her.* **Socks** *is bent and grey, her face rarely visible since she doesn't look into others' eyes. She has some teeth missing, and gives the impression of a person who* *has aged too quickly, who is really much younger than she appears. She speaks to no one in particular.*

Socks   I useta have kids. I had three and the welfare took two, I can't remember what happen to that other boy. His daddy! that's what, motherfucker fought for him then wouldn't let me come close. Yaw, shit! yaw should get a goddamn vacuum cleaner, how this thing s'posed to clean up all this shit? Damn, how many straws left in this fuckin' thing, three? Daddy, his goddamn motherfucker daddy took him. What was that motherfucker's name?

C.O. (*offstage*)   Get to work, Denise!

Denise (*mumbling to herself*)   I ain't workin' with that ol' crackhead, you must be outa your damn –

C.O.   WORK!

Denise, *angry, lazily pushes the broom, no rhyme or reason.*

Denise (*mumbling*) My shift over five minutes. What's the goddam point I start now? *hate* this fuckin' job! hate workin' with fuckin' addicts and AIDS	**Socks** Remember, runnin' he ram that nail up his foot? You say 'We take it out It be fine' Bullshit! I know what to do – emergency room: tetanus. What planet you on?

Denise (*uninterrupted, louder*)   *Shit*, Socks, you're sweepin' your goddamn dust on my toes!

Prix *enters.*

Denise   Glad you're here, relieve me, nothin' round here but fuckin' addicts and AIDS.

Prix *takes* **Denise**'s *broom, starts sweeping, ignores* **Denise**.

Denise   Aintchu lucky you got switched out the kitchen. This nuthouse crackhead, and guess who I was stuck with before her? *Socks! you sweep shit on my feet again I lay you out!* Some dumb ol' smack bitch, done the needle once too much now got the full-blown, this ain't a penal colony, it's a leper colony. (*Starts to leave.*)

C.O. (*offstage*)   Stay there, Denise.

Denise   *What?*

C.O.   *Stay there.*

Denise   Shit! What is it now? Guess I ain't worked hard enough for 'em guess they expect me to do some other goddamn job, I ain't no goddamn slave. (*Sits. Beat.*) You know two a the counselors quit. Just like the six others this year 'cept they ain't found a replacement yet, this means tomorrow's counselin' group got the goddamn adolescents mixed in, our nice quiet adult session have present the damn disruptin' brats.

C.O. (*offstage*)   Toilet cleanin'.

Denise (*to* **C.O.**, *incredulous*)   *Who?* (*Gets the answer.*) Fuck! Fuck fuck fuck!

Denise *exits.* **Socks** *and* **Prix** *push brooms in silence awhile. Eventually* **Prix** *absently sweeps near* **Socks**.

Socks   Outa here! Outa here! that's your place here's mine, I ain't come close to you, you don't come close to me! Space!

Socks *goes back to work, sweeping more rapidly than before.* **Prix** *stares at her, stunned.*

Prix   Malika?

Malika (**Socks**) *instantly stops pushing the broom, stares at* **Prix**, *terrified. Silence.*

Prix   Prix.

Malika *continues to stare at* **Prix**, *confused at to what to do.*

Malika   I gotta go to the bathroom. (*Pause.*) I GOTTA GO TO THE BATHROOM! I GOTTA GO TO THE

BATHROOM! I GOTTA GO TO THE BATHROOM! I
GOTTA GO –

C.O. (*entering*)   Okay, Socks, shut up!

C.O. *snatches* **Malika**'s *arm and starts to escort her off but*
Malika *pulls back.*

C.O.   Hey!

Malika *hesitantly touches the* **C.O.**'s *metal name pin, sees her
reflection in it. Glances in* **Prix**'s *direction without looking directly at*
Prix. *Exits with* **C.O.**

Scene Four

Prix *outside a closed bathroom door.*

Two teenagers – a **Girl** *and* **Pepper** *– enter, get in line behind*
Prix. **Prix** *in prison garb, the girls in street clothes.*

Pepper   She's all snotty, like, 'No one should be in here
for parole violation.' I'm like 'Mrs Garcia, I couldn't help
it.' She's like, 'That's stupid, Pepper, all you had to do was
show up four o'clock like you s'posed ta.' I'm like 'Bitch, you
know where the goddamn juvenile office is *Told*ja I be
crossin' lines get myself killed,' she's like, 'Thought you
weren't in it no more.' How stupid is she? Like just cuz I
decide to quit today the enemy conveniently get amnesia,
don't remember last week I was gang? Shit.

Girl   She just ain't gettin' it regular.

Both girls giggle.

Pepper   Fuck, you always say that.

Girl   The other day fiddlin' with her purse I saw her pull
out a condom. She put it back real fast hopin' no one
noticed.

Pepper   If she carryin' protection around I guess she
gettin' it regular.

Girl   Women gettin' it regular has their men carryin' it around. Woman gotta carry it herself just hopin' for a accidental emergency. (*They're laughing bigger.*) She know I saw too, I saw the look –

Jupiter *enters and the girls immediately fall to silence, not looking at each other. The door opens. A woman exits.* **Prix** *goes in, closing the door behind her. The lock clicks. The girls turn to* **Jupiter** *who gives them a look. One of the girls takes a paper clip and quickly jiggles the lock open. The two girls enter, shutting the door behind them. Sound: the girls punching and kicking the crap out of* **Prix**. *They have apparently gagged her so muffled struggle sounds may be heard from her but no screams.* **Jupiter**, *keeping watch outside, finally opens the door, allowing the audience to see, and enters.* **Prix** *being beaten severely.* **Jupiter** *observes the violence momentarily.*

Jupiter   Okay.

The violence ceases.

Jupiter   Liked your speech.

The girls giggle.

Prix (*struggling to speak*)   You didn't like it.

Jupiter   Pulled the heart, teared the eye. (*Long 'e' in 'teared'.*)

Prix *mumbles.*

Jupiter   WHAT?

Prix (*still struggling against the pain*)   Ancient. Years ago I wrote it, today remembered . . . few words, today . . . matters.

Jupiter   Matters to who? Pile a shit The Ladies liked it. The Ladies listen like you the prize poet Ladies The Ladies how the fuck old are ya ole ladies? Thirty?

Prix   Twenty-eight.

Jupiter (*puts the toilet lid down*)   Speak, Twenty-eight.

Prix   You're fourteen. I came to your christenin'.

Jupiter (*raises the toilet lid a bit, slams it down*)   Speak!

Prix (*struggles to stand on the toilet seat*)   The accepting, non-judgmental atmosphere of my group has allowed me to re-evaluate my choices . . . helped me to see my errors attributable to . . . to upbringing as well as personal choice sometimes . . . Sometimes I think if I had been shown one kindness . . .

Prix *stops.* **Pepper** *and the* **Girl**, *who had been rolling on the floor, gales of laughter, become quiet when they realize* **Prix** *has stopped.*

Girl   You didn't finish it.

Pepper (*more eager than unkind*)   Say the best part. Say it!

Prix (*gathers her strength*)   On this day . . . we are sisters –

Pepper/Girl (*whooping it up*)   'My sisters' 'My sisters'!

Jupiter *stares at* **Prix** *as the other girls roar. Suddenly she forces a mocking laugh.*

Jupiter   You say that so fuckin' serious like you believe that crap.

Long pause.

Prix   I don't.

Jupiter (*eyes still on* **Prix**)   Get the fuck outa here.

Pepper *and the* **Girl** *confused.* **Jupiter** *glares at them. They exit quick.*

Pepper   Sorry, Jupiter.

Jupiter   Get down.

Prix *steps down off the toilet.*

Jupiter   Usually I ain't s' hands off, don't order no one to kick the shit outa someone without I'm right there in with 'em, but doctor said I gotta watch the physical stuff. First trimester.

Prix   Sorry, Jupit –

Jupiter *snaps open the toilet, puts* **Prix**'s *head in and flushes several times. Snaps* **Prix**'s *head out and immediately pulls a razor from her own mouth, puts it against* **Prix**'s *throat.*

Prix (*choking*)   Your mother . . . Your mother –

Jupiter   My mother fuck! Like I ever see the bitch between jail and the fosters *good!* And each time I'm took away she wanna bawl and bawl like she so Christ fuckin' sad fuck her! Dontcha be mentionin' her fuckin' stupid name to me Don't be bringin' up no goddamn Comet!

Prix   Your third birthday, she show me the shoppin' bag. Pooh bear.

Jupiter *glaring at* **Prix**. *Then suddenly slams* **Prix**'s *head against the back of the toilet.*

Jupiter   Original Gangsta. (*Exits, laughing.*)

Scene Five

Picnic table.

Angel *clears the remnants of dinner. A pattern that repeats every few seconds:* **Prix** *looking into the sky,* **Angel** *looking at her watch,* **Prix** *looking at her watch.*

Angel   Few broken ribs. There was this blod clot, scared us awhile but then it cleared up. Told us they figure he be released Tuesday. (*To kids in distance.*) LET GO A HIM! HEY, HE WOULDN'TA BEEN DOIN' IT TO YOU IF YOU WEREN'T DOIN' IT TO HIM FIRST! And they still chargin' him, resistin' arrest, how the fuck when they ain't got a scratch and his body covered in blood? shit. I don't know why he don't get ridda that damn car anyway, he been stopped harrassed three times in four months ain't

he figured out yet cops don't like a black man drivin' that
make a car? GET DOWN! I TOLDJA STAY OUTA
THAT DAMN TREE! Guess your parole officer set you up,
some real excitin' job.

Prix   Burger King.

Angel   He ain't like you and me, my brothers . . . Like
Vince, total innocent, football, *a*s and *b*s then walk into
them drive-by bullets. And Darryl. Darryl ain't done a
wrong thing his whole life, nothin' but take care a his
girlfriend his kids, which what sent him to jail first time.
Illegal sale a food stamps ooh ain't they cheatin' on the
taxpayers, ain't the taxpayers so mad he cheated thirty
bucks this month feed his kids while business people writin'
off two hundred dollar lunches every fuckin' day a the week
but yeah, taxpayers pay that, that's fine, that's legal.

Prix   Clear night.

Angel   Worst is sentenced him to lifetime a welfare, every
time my baby brother try for employment, can't get past the
application question: 'You ever been convicted of a felony?'
Why you keep lookin' at your watch?!

Prix   Why you?

Angel   Somethin' up my sleeve *told*ja! Surprise!

Prix (*vague snicker, then*)   When?

Angel   Dontchu worry about it I'll letcha know. When it's
ready I'll letcha know. My question: what train you got to
catch?

Prix (*beat*)   Daily check-in. She said she be in the
neighborhood on the hour *don't be late*. If I get sent back sure
ain't be cuza violation a parole.

Angel   My plans!

Prix   Won't take more 'n a minute I ain't leavin'. (*Mutter-chuckle.*) Plans.

Beat.

Angel   Run into Comet the other day, supermarket. Big as
a house. Invite me to her baby shower, Sunday. Wanna go?

For the first time **Prix** *looks right at* **Angel**.

Prix   I ain't never in my life uttered a kind syllable to
Comet now why you think she want me at her shower?

Angel   You useta go to that shit. 'Free cake' you say.

Prix   Only invited cuza office politics, me her boss. Then.
(*Beat.*) Why you invite me to this? Your oldest fourth grade
and I ain't never bothered to meet none of 'em 'til today I
ain't exactly close family.

Angel   Third grade. My mother thought it be nice to ask,
havin' the picnic anyway why not make it a Welcome Home
Prix. She called to work, your mom's not feelin' well, all this
food . . . (*Beat.*) Didn't expect ya to accept. (*Chuckles.*) First
you don't. 'Prix, you liketa come?' 'No.' Thirty seconds you
call back, 'Yes. I'll bring some chocolate chips.' Why you
change your mind?

Prix   I dunno. Five weeks outa jail, somethin' to do 'sides
work. TV.

Angel (*beat.*)   Nice, delayin' things this year. Quiet. We in
this spot every Fourth – GIVE IT BACK! and the park wall
to wall packed. Not all bad the kids, chicken pox in bed over
the holiday, here we are now, space and peace. (**Angel** *takes
out a photograph, hands it to* **Prix**.) Happy Twenty-sixth a July.

Prix (*studies the photo*)   Where was *this*?

Angel   Our old old apartment. Don't remember it?

Prix *shakes her head no.*

Angel   We were six, first grade. Sonia was seven, Darryl
three. And Vince! All us standin' fronta the tree like we told
but big brother, Mr Independent, gotta be on the bike.

Prix   I remember those decorations. Yaw ever buy any new ones? Same ol' glitter bell, same ol' star. 'Cept . . . looks so new. (*Chuckles.*) Darryl! That baby grin, people always tellin' babies to smile, only thing they know how to do is show their teeth and grit 'em.

Angel   Like your smile was any realer. Prix the sad sack, even if we freeze tag even if we double-dutch you one a them kids always got somethin' unhappy behind all the giggle-play.

Prix (*studies the picture more closely*)   I'm smilin'.

Angel   Look at it.

Prix *studies the picture again. Now she sees it and, as best she can, suppresses the sudden, painful memory. Then looks at her watch.*

Prix   Time.

Prix *snatches her empty backpack, looping it on one shoulder, and quickly gets up to leave.*

Angel   I *knew* it! I *knew* it!

Prix   What?

Angel (*clutching part of the backpack*)   You makin' a connection! Month out and already you back. Not around my kids! I left it years ago, Prix, I grew up!

Prix (*mutters as she exits*)   You don't know what you're talkin' about.

Angel (*calling*)   Don't I? *I* learned somethin'! *I* learned somethin'! (*Starts clearing table again, slamming stuff.*) COME ON, YAW, WE LEAVIN'! (*Continues clearing. Then, aware the kids have ignored her.*) COME ON!

Prix *returns with a stuffed backpack.* **Angel** *sees.*

Angel   Fuck you, Prix! I don't *know* you Ain't settin' *me* up guilt by association GO! Bring that shit around my kids COME ON! Fuck you! Fuck you! Fuck –

Prix *has unzipped the bag for* **Angel** *to peer in.* **Angel** *does, and is surprised.* **Prix** *pulls out a rocket, touching it tenderly.*

Prix   I got it planned. This ain't the big show I always wanted, Class B, but I do okay with these home 'works, aerials and fountains and Roman candles, rockets, still meticulous with the color effects, style. Whole show won't be five minutes, I could drag it out make it last and everyone waitin', waitin' anticipatin' the next shell but the excitement, the euphoria is in the momentum don't drop it. I paint the emotional rhythms, some calmer than others these peaks and dips important to prevent monotony, just never let drop the thrill to nil.

Angel, *fascinated, has pulled out a few of the fireworks, looking them over.*

Angel   My kids regret I call they pay me no mine when I tell 'em what they missed. (*Still fascinated, then.*) Hey! These can't explode by touch can they? My hands kinda hot and sweaty ain't gonna light no fuse, right? Mushroom cloud?

Prix   When it's over . . . You ever see what it's like, enda the big Fourth show, East River? Two types a people. First is the two million who seen it, walkin' in a daze a beauty high. Harmony. Second is the people in the cars waitin' for the harmony heads-in-the-clouds people to cross the damn street, beepin' and all fury, impatient anyway but now hoppin' mad cuz they confused: How come pedestrians ain't gettin' mad right back? Cuz just when we thought couldn't get no more radiant no more splendorous than it already has it does, sometimes so high I wish it *would* stop, I think can't nobody stand this much . . . beauty? No. Ecstasy.

Prix *studies the sky. Then looks at* **Angel**.

Prix   Stand back.

Angel *exits.* **Prix** *walks around a bit, anxious, preparing herself. Then stoops. Lights a match. The fireworks. They last a few seconds with firecracker noise, and are suddenly done.* **Prix** *stares. Elation. Sound: slow squeaky wheels.* **Prix** *turns to look offstage to the* *approaching sound.* **Jo** *enters in a squeaky wheelchair. Slowly turning.* **Prix** *stares at her.*

Jo   You done it.

Prix *smiles. Then sees* **Jo***'s eyes, looks at the wheelchair. It dawns on her.* **Prix** *begins shaking her head.*

Prix   No . . .

Jo   YOU DONE IT!

Prix   NO! Done what? I don't know you!

Jo   You know me.

Prix   Don't!

Jo   YES!

Jo's Friend *(entering)*   C'mon, Jo.

Jo   She says she don't know me!

Jo's Friend   She knows you.

Prix   *I don't!*

Jo's Friend   *Bitch!* she knows!

Prix *vehemently shaking her head.*

Jo   You sixteen, me seventeen, the zoo.

Prix *blank.*

Jo   BRONX ZOO! REPTILES!

Prix   I DON'T REMEMBER!

Jo   She says she don't remember!

By now, **Angel** *has entered.*

Jo's Friend   Fucker!

Prix   I don't know, I don't –

Jo   She don't remember!

Jo's Friend   BITCH!

Prix   It mighta happened! I ain't sayin' it didn't happen, a lotta stuff . . . Long time ago, lotta stuff blur I don't remember it all! Lotta stuff I did. Don't remember it all!

Jo's friend *is wheeling* **Jo** *off.*

Prix   DON'T REMEMBER IT ALL!

Just before **Jo's Friend** *gets* **Jo** *off,* **Jo** *pushes* **Jo's Friend***'s hands away and, with great effort, turns 360 degrees around to face* **Prix***. She stares at* **Prix** *a long time, and* **Prix** *stares back until she can't stand it, looks away.*

Jo   This ain't the half of it.

Jo *turns back around, wheels herself off, accompanied by* **Jo's Friend***.* **Prix** *stares where they exited, then swings around to* **Angel***.*

Prix   I don't remember her! (**Angel** *says nothing.*) You know her? I don't! I don't remember her! (**Angel** *says nothing.*) It ain't s'posed to be like this! It ain't . . . if we had differences, gone! Gone, You ever see the Fourth, East River? *Every*body's happy, everybody, no anger! No anger! (*Beat.*) I didn't do 'em right. Maybe I done 'em wrong musta put the wrong colors together, clashed some colors dampered the emotional scheme WHAT'D I DO?

Pause.

Angel   It's ready. Come on.

Prix   You remember her?

Angel *shakes her head no.*

Prix   I know! I had two greens together, too much repetition too much cool. I fucked it up.

Angel   Maybe she just crazy.

Prix *turns to* **Angel** *quickly, this suggestion having given her great hope. Just as quickly she is disappointed to see in* **Angel***'s face that*

Angel *doesn't believe what she just said. Turns back to stare in the direction* **Jo** *exited.*

Prix   I ain't callin' her a liar just . . . (*Pause.*)

Angel (*exiting*)   Come on.

Prix *continues to stare after* **Jo**. *Finally she turns around.* **Angel** *is gone. Confused, she looks for* **Angel** *in the dark. In a narrow space,* **Prix** *is startled to find* **Angel** *and a hugely pregnant* **Comet**.

Prix   Comet . . .

Comet *gives* **Angel** *a look.* **Prix**, *suddenly feeling surrounded and terrified, gives an unconscious cry, backing up.* **Comet** *and* **Angel** *pull out from behind their backs several of* **Prix**'s *colored pen lights and form fireworks for* **Prix**. **Prix** *suppresses her sobs.*

Scene Six

34th and 5th Avenue.

Mother, *tired, weak, on the corner. The lights of the city reflect upon her – particularly, because she stands right in front of it, the blue and yellow of the Empire State Building.* **Prix** *enters. Her voice is flat, expressionless. If she has worried at all about her* **Mother**, *she conceals it well.*

Prix   What?

Mother (*pleased*)   Found me! (*The effort to speak sends her into a coughing fit.*)

Prix   Your goddamn note was pretty specific, 34th and 5th. Half expected to see your guts splattered where you're standin' why the hell else you be at the Empire State Buildin' midnight.

Mother   *Almost* midnight. Remember?

Prix *stares at her, still expressionless.*

Mother   Lights out! Midnight, they turn off the Empire State.

Prix   You come all the way down here for that.

Mother *grins.*

Prix   Let's go. (*Turns to leave.*)

Mother   *NO!* Wantchu to see.

Prix   I believe you, come on.

Mother   You don't believe me.

Prix   If ya gone to all the trouble a comin' down here to prove it must be true. Come on, we'll watch it on the way to the subway, you know they space the trains half-hour apart after twelve.

Mother *won't budge.*

Prix   They got me on the goddamn breakfast shift I gotta be there goddamn five a.m. prepare the goddamn powdered eggs and biscuits. We leave now and if the odds with us, no wait for the train, maybe we make it home by one, maybe I get a luxury three hours' sleep.

Mother   I hate they give you that job! That's parole board's idea a keepin' you outa jail, can't support yourself plus they know you got me, how they speck you to survive?

Prix (*more to herself*)   I found a little supplemental income.

Mother *scared.*

Prix   Don't flip I ain't in it no more just here and there: sell a few food stamps, bitta herb. Don't freak. Retired. Thirty pretty old to still bang in the gangs. (*Beat.*) How much longer?

Mother   Seconds.

Prix, *hands in jacket pockets, leans against a pole.*

Mother   What day's today? I mean, what's blue and yellow?

Prix   Nothin'.

Mother   Somethin'.

Prix   Nothin'. Red Valentine's, red and green Christmas, red white and blue Fourth, people start assumin' every Empire State color combo means somethin'. 'S arbitrary, every day ain't a holiday but Empire still gotta be lit.

Mother   'Til midnight.

Pause.

Mother   You ever thinka him?

Prix   Who?

Mother *looks at* **Prix**. *Now* **Prix** *understands who* **Mother** *means and is startled as she realizes she hasn't thought of him.*

Prix   No. No, useta. Useta think about him all the time. Not lately. Not in years.

Pause.

Mother   Different. Was a time you'da seen that note from me, tossed it in the trash, gone boutcher business. Seems you different all growed up, seems you ain't s' mad no more.

Prix *says nothing.*

Mother   These colors. They nice together?

Prix (*studies them*)   Blue and yellow, cool and warm. Sweet. Fireworks, blue's hardest color to mix.

Mother   Shoot. Nursin' a little bitta flu, 'f I'da known boutcher fireworks show . . .

Beat.

Prix   Didn't work out. Think I keep it a spectator sport from now on.

Mother   We go to the fireworks, I can't hardly look at
'em. Busy starin' at your face. The wonder, happy happy.
And best is when it's over, after the last big boom the
moment the lights all out, I see in your eyes a . . . sweetness.
Calm after the joy storm.

*The sixteen-note church bell hour tune begins, followed by the twelve
tolls. Soon after the tune starts,* **Prix** *speaks.*

Prix   Midnight.

Mother   Wait.

They watch in silence a few moments.

Mother   Prix. What happen to all your artwork?
Fireworks things.

Prix   Angel saved the pen lights. Rest got lost or thrown
out while I was in jail.

Mother   Them figures? Pipe cleaners?

Prix   Gone.

Mother   Useta always be new ones, you constant
recreatin'. How come you ain't replaced 'em? I don't ever
see ya doin' your sketches no more, that was your one thing,
one thing hope you ain't lost interest. (**Prix** *says nothing.*) I
wisht I'da kept one. Wisht you still made 'em pipe cleaner
figures I wisht I had one for me. (*Pause.*) Prix. I know . . . I
know you ain't much into grantin' favors but . . . (*Pulls much
change from her pocket.*) I found some money today, I thought –

Prix   I toldju not to do that! Panhandlin', Jesus! we ain't
fuckin' beggars!

Mother   I just thought, maybe you can't afford the pipe
cleaners, maybe that why you don't do it no more.

Prix   Do I look like I got time to fool around, arts and
crafts? Grown woman.

Beat. Then **Mother** *holds out coins to* **Prix**.

Mother   Prix. You make one? For me?

Prix, *pointedly looking at the building and not at her* **Mother**, *shakes her head no.* **Mother** *stares. Then, sudden and desperate:*

Mother   PRIX! YOU MAKE ONE? FOR ME?

The force of her emotion causes **Mother** *to drop her coins. She falls to her knees to pick them up.* **Prix** *starts to help but* **Mother** *violently waves her away.* **Prix** *gazes at her* **Mother**, *for the first time in the play really seeing her.* **Mother** *gathers most of the money, then stops. Just after the twelfth bell toll (the elongated reverberations or increased volume should indicate its finality)* **Mother** *lifts her face to look at* **Prix**.

Prix   Yes.

The lights of the Empire State Building go out.

Methuen Modern Plays
include work by

Methuen Contemporary Dramatists
include

Peter Barnes (three volumes)
Sebastian Barry
Edward Bond (six volumes)
Howard Brenton
  (two volumes)
Richard Cameron
Jim Cartwright
Caryl Churchill (two volumes)
Sarah Daniels (two volumes)
Nick Darke
David Edgar (three volumes)
Ben Elton
Dario Fo (two volumes)
Michael Frayn (two volumes)
Paul Godfrey
John Guare
Peter Handke
Jonathan Harvey
Declan Hughes
Terry Johnson (two volumes)
Bernard-Marie Koltès
David Lan
Bryony Lavery
Doug Lucie
David Mamet (three volumes)

Martin McDonagh
Duncan McLean
Anthony Minghella
  (two volumes)
Tom Murphy (four volumes)
Phyllis Nagy
Anthony Nielsen
Philip Osment
Louise Page
Joe Penhall
Stephen Poliakoff
  (three volumes)
Christina Reid
Philip Ridley
Willy Russell
Ntozake Shange
Sam Shepard (two volumes)
Wole Soyinka (two volumes)
David Storey (three volumes)
Sue Townsend
Michel Vinaver (two volumes)
Michael Wilcox
David Wood (two volumes)
Victoria Wood

Methuen World Classics
include

Jean Anouilh (two volumes)
John Arden (two volumes)
Arden & D'Arcy
Brendan Behan
Aphra Behn
Bertolt Brecht (six volumes)
Büchner
Bulgakov
Calderón
Čapek
Anton Chekhov
Noël Coward (seven volumes)
Eduardo De Filippo
Max Frisch
John Galsworthy
Gogol
Gorky
Harley Granville Barker
  (two volumes)
Henrik Ibsen (six volumes)
Lorca (three volumes)

Marivaux
Mustapha Matura
David Mercer (two volumes)
Arthur Miller (five volumes)
Molière
Musset
Peter Nichols (two volumes)
Clifford Odets
Joe Orton
A. W. Pinero
Luigi Pirandello
Terence Rattigan
  (two volumes)
W. Somerset Maugham
  (two volumes)
August Strindberg
  (three volumes)
J. M. Synge
Ramón del Valle-Inclán
Frank Wedekind
Oscar Wilde

Methuen Student Editions

John Arden	*Serjeant Musgrave's Dance*
Alan Ayckbourn	*Confusions*
Aphra Behn	*The Rover*
Edward Bond	*Lear*
Bertolt Brecht	*The Caucasian Chalk Circle*
	Life of Galileo
	Mother Courage and her Children
Anton Chekhov	*The Cherry Orchard*
Caryl Churchill	*Top Girls*
Shelagh Delaney	*A Taste of Honey*
John Galsworthy	*Strife*
Robert Holman	*Across Oka*
Henrik Ibsen	*A Doll's House*
Charlotte Keatley	*My Mother Said I Never Should*
Bernard Kops	*Dreams of Anne Frank*
Federico García Lorca	*Blood Wedding*
	The House of Bernarda Alba
	(bilingual edition)
John Marston	*The Malcontent*
Willy Russell	*Blood Brothers*
Wole Soyinka	*Death and the King's Horseman*
August Strindberg	*The Father*
J. M. Synge	*The Playboy of the Western World*
Oscar Wilde	*The Importance of Being Earnest*
Tennessee Williams	*A Streetcar Named Desire*
Timberlake Wertenbaker	*Our Country's Good*